SCM PA

recent titles include

L. ALETRINO

Six World Religions

SCM PRESS LTD
BLOOMSBURY STREET LONDON

Translated by Mary Foran from the third Dutch edition
Zes Wereldgodsdiensten
Scheltema & Holkema N.V., Amsterdam, 1967

S B N 334 01532 4
First published 1968
© *SCM Press Ltd* 1968
Printed in Great Britain by
Billing & Sons Limited
Guildford and London

CONTENTS

CONTENTS

INTRODUCTION

IN THE confused times in which we live it is a pleasant and refreshing task to explore the religions which originated in the distant past and which, up to the present day, have attracted millions of people. All religions, in the form they have acquired in the course of time, reflect man's ideals and interpret his emotional desires. All these religions have certain points in common. They are, to a certain extent, complementary and have in many a period formed the goal of 'the Pilgrimage of Mankind'. The history of the various religions, however, is not composed entirely of stimulating and uplifting episodes. The contrasts between them have repeatedly led to strife and much blood has flowed.

It may well be said that the structure and aims of the religions, as practised today, do not always correspond to the intentions of their founders. Their form has for the most part been determined by disciples of these founders, and there is often a great gulf to be discerned between the original aim and the later development. God's word has not infrequently been considerably changed by human hands, and much that is human – only too human in fact – has crept in. Ideas too have changed with the passing of time, and religions have adapted themselves to the times.

Despite all their differences, however, and even their hostility, all religions have this in common: man's relationship to God or to a being revered as divine, an impersonal power of a different nature from man. Even where the existence of God is expressly denied one can still speak of man's relationship to something which he cannot explain in terms of himself or of known phenomena, but which he wishes to love, to fear and to serve.

In this book we have attempted to give an outline of a number of the most important non-Christian world religions, sketching their origin, meaning, nature, growth and – where relevant – decline, without venturing to pass judgment on whether or not they are 'true'. Our book is deliberately incomplete, in the sense that we make no attempt to compete with the numerous scholars, theologians and religious historians from whose recognized standard works we have derived some of our information. Our study is intended for those interested readers who have indeed heard of Islam, Buddhism, Brahmanism, Hinduism, Shintoism and Judaism, but whose knowledge is perhaps limited to the chief characteristics of these religions since they have had insufficient opportunity to explore the history of their origin and development.

Of the two possible ways of dealing with religion, from the point of view of faith or from that of history, we have chosen the second. We have examined our subjects as cultural phenomena, and described them as historical phenomena. From time to time this necessarily involved penetrating to the heart of the religion under discussion in order to be able to understand the meaning of its outward manifestations. This led us back to the depths of man's own nature, where he finds contact with the only and eternal source of his existence. More than ever we become conscious of the sameness of all religions and of the arrogance of those who do not believe in the faith of those whose belief differs from their own. We are therefore all the more pleased to note the recent development in the West of a more open-minded attitude towards the non-Christian world religions and the beginnings of a mutual exchange of ideas (in, for example, the World Congress of Faiths).

We felt it necessary to submit each of these studies to an expert in order to be sure that our remarks on the actual data and our interpretation of particular doctrines were correct. We should therefore like to express our gratitude in the first place to Mr A. Schuster, Chief Rabbi of the Netherlands-Israelite Community in Amsterdam, whose dedication and broad critical sense were a great comfort and support to us; also to Professor Dr C. C. Kreiger, formerly professor in the Japanese language and ethnology at the University of Utrecht, to Dr F. Vos, lecturer in Japanese at Leiden, to Dr R. L. Mellema of the Royal Tropical Institute and to Mrs M. A. Spruitenburg-Dwars of Huizen. We are extremely grateful to all of them for the interest they have shown in our work and for the care with which they read the chapter on their particular subject in order to give us the benefit of their suggestions. Naturally they accept no responsibility for the views and judgments of the present author.

On consulting the numerous sources we were struck by the fact that varying, even contradictory, opinions and interpretations exist among the experts on points of fundamental importance. This, however, is not uncommon in the domain of scholarship.

1

ISLAM

ISLAM IS by far the most recent of the non-Christian world religions. It dates from the beginning of the seventh century of our era so that one is not obliged to grope in the dark for information concerning its origin and expansion; a number of well-nigh inexhaustible sources may be consulted.

Islam is the religion of Muhammad. The word *Islam* (*aslama*) already existed before Muhammad: it is of Arabic origin and means 'complete submission' (subjection) to *Allah*, the one God. The word Allah, too, is Arabic, a contraction of Al-Ilah, 'the God'. The veneration of Allah was already known outside Islam, but it was the revelations granted to the prophet Muhammad which led to Allah's becoming the monotheistic God of Islam and as such the central figure in the Qur'ān. The word used to describe the adherents of Islam are Muslim or Moslem ('he who submits').

Islam comprises a great diversity of races. It originated among the Arabs and spread to the Persians, Caucasians, Turks, Egyptians, Berbers, Tartars, Chinese and Indonesians. The largest group of supporters may be found today in India and Pakistan, roughly one-hundred million of them. Islam owes its unity and political power to the successors of Muhammad who waged wars of conquest under religious banners, not unconnected with the existing economic urge to expand. In this respect Islam was no different from the many other religions which sought to impose their beliefs through fire and the sword. However, these wars of conquest of the Muslim rulers were aimed exclusively at extending their political power. They preferred the subject peoples to retain their own beliefs, since this was not without advantage to the Muslim state. The inhabitants of a non-Muslim subject state were relegated to the status of second-class citizens; they were not allowed to hold office or to serve in the army and were obliged to pay an annual poll-tax to the treasury. However, once the population became better acquainted with Islam and realized what the advantages of being Muslim are, many voluntarily embraced the new religion. This *voluntary* conversion was required by the Qur'ān. Several passages of the Qur'ān expressly prohibit any forcible interference with religious liberty ('There may be no compulsion in religion'), while complete tolerance is one of the basic principles of Islam. Islam, however, does preach the *jihad* (holy war). Three categories are distinguished: the little *jihad*, i.e. war against an attacker in defence of one's own religious liberty; the great *jihad*, the obligation of every Muslim to help in the spread of Islam wherever possible, though only peaceably and without coercion; and the greatest *jihad*, the struggle against oneself, submission in the profoundest sense of the word, the suppression of the ego. The Muslim is allowed to wage war on the following conditions: only when he is attacked, only against those who fight him, only within the limits of strict necessity, and only against soldiers. It is forbidden to carry the fight into any place used to perform religious ceremonies, unless forced to do so by the enemy. The struggle may continue only until freedom of religion and conscience are guaranteed; should the enemy desire peace it must be granted, otherwise the Muslims would then be the attackers. Yet despite these rules and all other regulations dealing with matters pertaining to war which are meticulously noted down in the Qur'ān, the question remains: how must one decide when a war is 'imposed' and when it is not? Throughout the entire history of the world, those who wage war have always called the opposing side 'attackers' and complained of a war 'imposed' upon them. The Muslims go even further: for them the earth is divided into Muslim territory (Dar al-Islam) and 'battle territory'. During Muhammad's lifetime the prophet is said to have been frequently informed by Allah when he should wage war in order to protect Islam, a (political) religious standpoint viewed with some reservation by the sceptical Westerner.

Religious historians differ in their opinion of the reliability of the available data on the life of Muhammad, especially his early years. One may consider that we possess complete information which has been proved accurate, while another holds that much apocryphal matter has crept into the description of his personality during the course of time. Muslim scholars and graphologists, and Western orientalists attracted to Islam or who have embraced the religion of Islam, reproach non-Muslim theologians and men of letters with viewing Islam too much from the standpoint of the Western Christianity, and accuse them of clinging to certain prejudices.

Muhammad (*al-Amin*, the faithful) is usually held to have been born in A.D. 571. He belonged to a branch of Quraysh, the Hashimites, the guardians of the Kaaba, the Sacred House and spiritual centre in Mecca. His father Abd-allah had died before he was born and his mother Amina died while he was still a young boy. Abd al-Moettalib, his grandfather, took charge of him and reared him until his uncle Abu Talib took over this task. There was nothing to indicate the magnificent destiny reserved for the young Muhammad. He chose trade as his profession and entered the service of a rich merchant's widow, Khadija, whom he married at the age of twenty-five. Several children were born of this union, including a daughter Fatima who was to become one of his most ardent disciples.

During Muhammad's boyhood and youth Mecca was a flourishing caravan town; its prosperous citizens made a good living from the transit trade between the Indian Ocean and the Mediterranean Sea. Like the Dutch or English seafarers of former centuries the inhabitants of Mecca possessed a certain cosmopolitan outlook. They were as much at home with primitive tribal chiefs as with high-placed foreign authorities, and were intellectually superior to the Arabs in many other centres. On the other side of the coin, the commercial prosperity of the city had given rise to social abuses; on the one hand wealth and luxury, on the other bitter poverty and an underworld of slaves and beggars. It is certain that these social evils and the prevailing moral corruption provoked the disgust and the revolt which inspired Muhammad. He did not, however, preach a social revolution. It was rather a religious inspiration which led him to accept a faith and an attitude to life which developed into a doctrine.

Was Muhammad, who possessed an oriental force of imagination and a profound seer's insight, really granted 'Apparitions' and 'Revelations'? It is said that the angel Gabriel appeared to him three times in a cave in the mountain of Hura, near Mecca. The terms in which the Revelations were formulated acquired for Muhammad the character of a divine Revelation which transformed him into the Messenger of Allah. Only at the cost of considerable inner searchings and anguish of soul did he come to believe that Allah had chosen him and no other as his ambassador on earth. The angel Gabriel revealed to him thoughts and precepts which are set down in the Qur'ān, the Sacred Book, thought to contain Allah's own words. The word Koran means recitation or 'that which must be recited'.

A distinction is made between the words spoken by Muhammad as Revelations and the ordinary precepts which he taught. The first are incorporated in the Qur'ān, the second form the body of the Hadith (Tradition). Except for the first occasion Muhammad is said never to have been alone when he received a Revelation. He was usually surrounded by friends who acted as witnesses. By no means all of them were literate, but it is well known that the Arab of that time possessed an exceptionally retentive memory, so that the Revelations, once heard, were remembered. Those who could write noted down the texts. Later Muhammad employed a scribe, who carefully wrote down all the Revelations. After Muhammad's death he gathered together all that had been revealed in the course of thirty-three years and handed it on to Muhammad's successor, Abu Bekr. Others, too, had independently taken note of the sayings of the Prophet. These were so important that they were handed down from generation to generation and formed the basis of the Hadith. Naturally enough comparison revealed differences in pronunciation and in vowel signs; the third Caliph, Othman, called together a number of scholars, among whom were contemporaries of Muhammad, and they established the definitive text. One result of this was that in later times, even in the most heated theological disputes, the authenticity and accuracy of the Qur'ān text were never questioned. The text, once codified, was beyond dispute.

The Qur'ān thus contains the words as revealed to Muhammad. It is not the repository of his own ideas. The Revelations, however, were not concerned exclusively with religious matters; they also dealt with the settling of differences in civil society and with regulations governing criminal law, trade and other matters. The Qur'ān is composed of 114 *suras* (chapters), divided into verses written in rhyming prose. The opening chapter contains only seven verses in which Allah answers questions dealing with the composition of the universe, the origin and destiny of the visible world and what lies hidden behind it.

The Muslims consider the Qur'ān as proof of Muhammad's divine mission. Just as the Torah was granted to Moses through divine inspiration, so, too, Muhammad received the inspirations which are set down in the Qur'ān. In the field of religious education it is well known how much stress is laid in Muslim countries on learning the whole of the text of the sacred Qur'ān by heart, and many indeed have succeeded in doing so. The Qur'ān is considered the unimpeachable source for the so-called 'moral duties' and the explanation of the theological dogmas, yet the methods of interpretation applied differ widely as a result of the various attitudes and trends which have grown up in Islam. The study of the Qur'ān thus also requires a sound knowledge of the numerous commentaries and interpretations. Independent interpretation is not permitted although, just as with the interpretation of the Bible, modernistic schools of thought would prefer to interpret the Qur'ān in the spirit of the forms and modes of thought of modern society. Like the Bible, the Qur'ān is regarded with the greatest reverence. Every title page of one eastern edition has the words 'only to be touched in a state of ritual purity'.

Muhammad's receptiveness to divine Revelations may be explained by the fact that he had long opposed the idolatry of his fellow citizens in Mecca, which was often accompanied by repulsive and immoral ceremonies. This idolatry had assumed such proportions that boulders, trees and heaps of sand were venerated and many families kept their own idols. Muhammad found support among numerous people who, probably under the influence of Christianity, aspired to a purer form of religious worship. At the outset it was his revolt against the religious practices and way of life of his fellow citizens that drove Muhammad, almost in spite of himself, in a direction which would finally lead to the emergence of Islam as a new religious community with its own religious characteristics and institutions. From time immemorial polytheism had held sway in Arabia, associated with the worship of the stars. Muhammad wished to return to the original faith as revealed, pure and untainted, by God, before it became obscured and bastardized by various additions. Islam, indeed, is often called the Arabic Protestantism of the seventh century.

The inhabitants of Mecca fiercely resisted the new teaching, more for political and economic reasons than for any well-considered disbelief in the doctrines preached. They feared the possible effect of Muhammad's monotheism on the financial profits from their holy places and realized that Muhammad's preaching could lead to the emergence of an immense political power in their oligarchic community.

For thirteen years Muhammad sought to combat resistance in Mecca, but with little success. He had the support of a small group of devoted adherents but the new doctrine made scarcely any progress. His opponents even disputed his claim to be a prophet; they demanded that he should work miracles as Isa (the Muslim name for Jesus) had done before him. Muhammad was unable to comply. He called the Qur'ān itself the greatest miracle and described it as the first writing present with Allah in heaven, the 'Mother of the Book', parts of which had also been revealed to Moses and to Jesus, destined for their peoples. None the less Muhammad was conscious that he had reached a dead end and he decided to transfer his work of conversion to a different field. This was a momentous decision, since his doctrine was practically unknown outside Mecca. He was sustained, however, by the example of the Bible. Just as Noah and his family had been compelled to take refuge in the Ark so that the Deluge might begin, and just as Moses and his people had had to leave Egypt so that God's judgment could be carried out, so ought he and his small band of followers to leave Mecca in order to make room for God's work in this obdurate city. Up till this time he had stood in Allah's way and prevented him from showing his might. Now, at ten days' journey from Mecca, lay the city of Medina which had been plagued for years by civil war between various Arab tribes. But the inhabitants were growing weary, and furthermore they feared that their weakness would be exploited by Jewish tribes. They therefore called upon Muhammad, who was reputed to be an honest and upright man, to act as arbiter and peacemaker. Muhammad hesitated a long time, for the negotiations about his coming lasted for over a year. However, having stipulated certain conditions regarding his own safety and that of his followers, he left Mecca secretly in the summer of 622 and went to Medina.

This 'migration', Hijra (not a 'flight' as it is generally considered, but a voluntary decision), is regarded as the starting-point of the expansion of Islam. In any case the Muslim era begins on this date, 16 July 622. (The Muslim year has twelve months; each month begins with the appearance of the new moon, so that the year numbers only 354 or 355 days.) With Muhammad's arrival at Medina the Islamic movement acquired a new form, being now a clearly defined community under one leader. Since Medina had turned to Muhammad and not vice versa, this was taken by Muhammad and his followers as a clear sign of Allah's support.

Muhammad's concern now was to invest his community with worldly authority. Medina, which had formerly been known as Jathrib, was given the name Madinat al-Nabi, the City of the Prophet, later transformed into Medina. Nor was it long before Muhammad acquired undisputed authority in his ever-growing community. The nature of his Revelations changed; they were no longer couched in prophetic terms, but became more down to earth and more concerned with social issues. Social and religious obligations were laid upon the community, among the principal requirements being obedience to Allah and to his Prophet. The slogan: 'Allah is most great. I testify that there is no God but Allah. I testify that Muhammad is God's apostle' became the basis of a religious doctrine which in its turn formed the foundation of a theocratic state. The Jewish and

Christian inhabitants of Mecca, it is true, rejected Muhammad's teaching, whereupon Muhammad dismissed the sacred Books of the Jewish and Christian communities as forgeries.

And yet Muhammad continued to be haunted by the city of Mecca which had 'cast him out' and thus rejected his divine doctrine. He desired to gain her in Allah's name; since the opposition of the Meccans was partly inspired by political and economic motives he would try a spiritual approach. A year after the 'migration' he proclaimed Mecca a 'Holy Place' with the Kaaba as its centre. This was an existing cube-shaped structure, said to have been built by Adam, destroyed by the Deluge, and rebuilt by Abraham at Allah's command. On top of this stood the various idols adored by the tribes. These idols were only removed eight years later when polytheism was abolished.

Yet, so long as Mecca remained hostile to the Islamic community, this community was in danger, for no place in western Arabia had so strong an intellectual and political élite, the ruling power. Muhammad must have foreseen that any attempt to convert (or to force) Mecca to Islam was bound to end in armed conflict, for he immediately set about reinforcing the inner and outer resistance of his community. By about the year 624 this was considered satisfactory enough to justify an attack upon Mecca. In a battle near Badr, to the south-west of Medina, a small force of Meccans was defeated; later the fortunes of war were reversed, and the Muslims suffered defeat near Mount Uhud at the hands of a punitive expedition from Mecca, which comprised not only Meccans but also Bedouin tribes. In 627 began the siege of Medina, which was surrounded by a rampart. The undertaking failed. Muhammad now decided that the time had come to march on Mecca with his troops. He found the city completely deserted, the inhabitants having fled to the mountains. The Meccans' military leaders surrendered, and Muhammad, riding his favourite camel Al-Kaswa, entered the city. He had given his soldiers strict orders neither to plunder nor to pillage. When the inhabitants heard how he had proceeded calmly and with dignity to the Sacred Temple in order to conduct a service there, they returned and recognized Muhammad as their spiritual leader. His power, both in religion and in politics, was now definitely established.

From this time onwards the Islamic movement became increasingly identified with the religious convictions prevailing in the Arab world. Despite his growing influence Muhammad did not lack opponents and he was obliged to use force against the tribes and groups which menaced his authority. The dispersal and extermination of Jewish tribes and settlements led to bloody excesses, and many of the Bedouin tribes were decimated. Violence reigned. Muhammad urged the Persian 'King of Kings', Chosroes III, the King of Egypt, the Negus of Abyssinia, and the Byzantine Emperor to accept Islam and to propagate it. To Heraclitus, the Roman Emperor, he wrote: 'Peace be to those who have followed the right road. I call you to Islam. Embrace Islam and God will reward you twofold. But woe to you if you refuse!' (This last threatening statement must be interpreted as 'Then fear God'.) This haughty tone and the later rapid spread of Islam as the result of political expansion have caused Muhammad to be considered by many as a 'false prophet', as a crafty demagogue interested only in political power. This view is still current in various Christian circles. Yet does not Jesus also say in the Gospel of John: 'I am the Way, the Truth and the Life'?

In March 632 Muhammad, feeling that death was near, undertook his historical farewell pilgrimage to the Kaaba in Mecca, where he revealed the ritual which was henceforth to be followed in the *hajj* (pilgrimage). He addressed a last message to his disciples, which concluded with the exhortations: 'Preserve the faith, since it is the will of Allah; be kind to the poor; give the labourer his wages before the sweat of his brow has dried; know that every true believer is the brother of every other true believer. We are all of the same quality; you are all members of one brotherhood.' He then returned to Medina where he died on 8 June 632 in his sixty-first year. He was buried in Medina. Very many of his followers refused to believe that he had left them for good until Abu Bekr, his confidant and successor, proclaimed: 'He who honours Muhammad, tell him that Muhammad is dead, but he who honours Allah, tell him that Allah lives and will not die.'

Up till now we have confined ourselves to sketching in broad outline the nature and origin of Islam, mentioning the principal facts from Muhammad's life. Now, however, we shall attempt to penetrate deeper to the heart of his religious doctrine.

This religious doctrine is based on the certainty that man is responsible to God for his acts. This responsibility extends over the frontier of his life and ends with death. God exists from all eternity. He is the only reality.

Although one seeks in vain in the Qur'ān for a systematic exposition of the Muslim faith, it does contain a clearly defined system of precepts. The words occurring in the fourth chapter (line 136) may be considered as the credo: 'O you, who believe, believe in God and his Apostle and in the Book which he has sent to his Apostle. He who denies God and his angels and his Books and the Last Days has strayed from the truth.' This credo is expressed in the above-mentioned profession of faith: *la ilaha illa'llah wa muhammadun rasulu'llah* (There is no God but Allah, and Muhammad is his apostle.) Muhammad imparted new meaning to the belief in one supreme God; he purified it of the elements of polytheism which had always clung to it, substituting a belief in a real, albeit supernatural Being, Creator and Sustainer of the Universe, the omniscient and almighty Arbiter of good and evil and the highest Judge of all mankind.

The angels are depicted in the Qur'ān as God's messengers. They are, like men, his creatures and servants. They record men's deeds, receive men's souls when they die, testify for or against them at the Last Judgment and guard the gates of hell. The figure of Satan (Iblis) does not represent the evil spirit, as with Christianity, but the angel who has revolted against God.

The Last Judgment, which occupied such an important place in Muhammad's thought and in the imagination of his followers, is represented as a cataclysm occurring at a time known only to God. Then the trumpet will sound, the heavens will open, and the mountains crumble. The graves will give up their dead, and the people will be called to give account. Each guardian angel will testify to the deeds of his charge, and these testimonies will then be weighed in the scales. Then the blessed, the godfearing, the humble and the charitable, the magnanimous and those who have suffered and have been persecuted for God's sake will be summoned to enter the garden of Eden, the abode of peace. Here they will dwell for ever, praising God, enjoying an abundance of food and drink, in the company of virgins and women of absolute purity. They will enjoy greater bliss than any earthly mortal has ever known.

But the sinners, the unbelievers and those who adore other gods than Allah will be cast into Purgatory, to suffer unrelieved torments. And these torments are severe, although the Qur'ān somewhat mollifies this horrifying picture of the sinner's end by repeated reassurances concerning the existence of Divine Grace and the possibility of God's intervention in favour of those in whom he is well pleased. Modern Islam teaches that man does not remain in the 'Fire' for ever; it must be viewed solely as a purification.

The doctrine of the Last Judgment occupies a prominent place in Muhammad's teaching. It has no basis in Arab thought but is derived from Christianity. Indeed, not only the ideas concerning the resurrection and the hereafter, but also many of the concepts regarding the joys of paradise and the torments of hell, have their parallels in the writings of the Christian church fathers and monks. The Muslims consider Judaism, Christianity and Islam as three forms of the same religion which in its original purity was the religion of Abraham: the offering of oneself to the will of God. For Muhammad the true believer was characterized by his ever-present fear of God. For God is the Almighty Lord, and man is his creation who is always in danger of arousing his wrath. Forgiveness may be obtained through the grace of God; man cannot earn it through his own merits, for then it would cease to be grace. In the Qur'ān, however, he can find the right road which will lead him to the highest good; he is required to serve God by means of good works and in particular through prayer and the giving of alms. This forms, as it were, the basis of all Muslim theology and ethics. Many of these elements are to be found in the

Christian religion and in various religious sects; good works, for example, among the Roman Catholics and the Mormons, and the expectation of the Last Judgment among the Jehovah's Witnesses.

Muhammad, however, did not confine himself to preaching the doctrine of an almighty and awful God. He also preached the gospel of hope, and, as the community grew, more stress was laid upon God's grace and mercy. God was even given a name which, to judge from the old, pre-Islamic, inscriptions, must have been very widespread in Arabia: *Ar Rahman*, the merciful God. This appellation also introduces every chapter of the Qur'ān: 'In the name of Allah, the compassionate. the merciful.'

Besides its religious doctrine, Islam also has a doctrine of moral duties. The religious doctrine is usually bound up with the first of the five principal duties of moral doctrine (Five Pillars or Foundations): (1) the *sahada* (confession of faith) ('There is no God but Allah' . . .), (2) the *salaat* (ritual-prayer exercises), (3) the *zakaat* (the performance of good works and almsgiving), (4) the fast, and (5) the once in a lifetime *hajj* (pilgrimage) to Mecca, whenever the required conditions can be satisfied.

The strict observance of the ritual prayers is considered as one of the essential duties of the Muslims. According to Sir Hamilton A. R. Gibb, whose 'historical survey' of Islam has virtually become a standard work (see p. 39), it is certain that the five prayer-periods of Islam were already established before Muhammad's death. The faithful are called to prayer by the *muezzin*, whose special task this is and who employs fixed formulas. He repeats four times the *Allahu Akbar* (God is most great), followed by 'I testify that there is no other God but Allah' (twice). Then comes: 'I testify that Muhammad is the apostle of Allah' (also twice) followed by 'Come to prayer' (twice), 'Come to salvation' (twice) and 'There is no God but Allah'. The morning *salaat* concludes with 'Prayer is better than sleep'. The first to make this call to prayer was Muhammad's Abyssinian slave Bilal.

On hearing the first words of the call to prayer, every Muslim stands, wherever he may be, and says the prayers with the prescribed ritual. The prayer should preferably be said in community, in a mosque or other 'place of prayer' and led by an Imam who stands before the faithful and indicates the proper time for each movement. This leader is not a priest. Islam has no mediating priesthood or earthly pastors; the Muslim is personally accountable to God for his deeds. There are, however, leaders who are chosen from the community for their knowledge of the Qur'ān and for their piety.

Before performing the *salaat* the believer must fulfil certain conditions. He must, among other things, be in a state of ritual purity which may be attained by certain ceremonial ablutions. When praying, the worshipper has his face turned towards Mecca. Every mosque, in no matter what part of the world, is built in such a way that the prayer recess (*mihrab*) points as nearly as possible in the direction of Mecca. The prayer begins with the raising of the hands to shoulder height and the pronouncing of the words *Allahu Akbar* (God is most great). The hands are then lowered, with the left hand folded within the right, and the first chapter, Opening (*Fatiha*), of the Qur'ān is recited. The worshipper then bends forward from the hips, with the hands resting on the knees. Next he straightens up, then sinking back on his knees, he places his hands and then his face on the ground while reciting the prayers. At each change of position the *Allahu Akbar* is said. There are five fixed periods for prayer: shortly before daybreak, at noon, in the middle of the afternoon, directly after sunset and in the first part of the night.

Allah has no need of prayer, said Muhammad; it is we ourselves who cannot do without it, since it is a means of bringing us closer to our goal: union with Allah. If all people were to come together and exert themselves to display the glory of God and to honour and praise him on this account, this would add nothing to his greatness. Still less would it detract from his greatness if all men were to gather together and deny it. Only through voluntary prayer can men obtain the Almighty's self-manifestation in the person praying. The prayer of the Muslim signifies the recognition of the greatness and glory of God. He does not ask for earthly things, for food and drink, for God grants these to everyone whether they adore him or not. He has

created everything and therefore he ('the Sustainer of all
things') supplies our needs.

The *zakaat* (good works and almsgiving) is considered as the
outward sign of piety. Just as the *salaat* is a duty towards God,
the *zakaat* is a duty towards one's fellow men, not a contribu-
tion or church tax, but a tax levied on the 'haves' for the benefit
of the 'have-nots'. It is considered as a 'loan' to God which
will be repaid with interest.

Fasting, which forms such an important part of the religious
life of the Muslim, occurs in the month of Ramadan, the ninth
month of the lunar year. It is considered the most sacred month,
since it was then that Muhammad received his first Revelations.
Fasting entails abstaining from food and sexual intercourse
between sunrise and sunset. During the whole of Ramadan
various public and private activities come to a halt and the
people spend a great part of the day resting, reciting from the
Qur'ān and attending special religious exercises. During this
time the Muslim must try to attain a higher level of virtue and
purity.

The sobriety of the Muslim way of life is based on 'Revelations' from which it is derived to become a sacred law. It is
accepted that this was so desired by Allah. The ban on drinking
wine or other alcoholic beverages, eating pork or the flesh of
animals not ritually slaughtered, using certain musical instruments or wearing silken clothes or gold ornaments (this applies
only to men) is based upon a Revelation of the Qur'ān. Man,
for Islam, is a psycho-physical unit. All that one absorbs, both
food and drink, influences body and spirit. The spirit cannot be
detached from the body, and one cannot entirely discount the
influence which physical make-up and outward conduct exercise upon the spirit. The body, accordingly, may not be neg-
lected at the expense of the spirit or vice versa. By following the
commandments and prohibitions of Islam man is able to raise
himself above the animal state and control his passions and
desires.

For, according to Muhammad's teaching, man is born without sin; he is thus not burdened with original sin. Unfortunately
he is often enticed by the beautiful appearance of worldly life;
he is deformed by his environment; and he falls into a deep pit.

Man is by nature pure and wholesome at birth. Islam leads man from his primitive human existence to a moral human existence. The Qur'ān shows how man must act in order to attain a high moral standard. Once this is achieved man must rise even higher from the moral to the spiritual plane. For our earthly existence is not aimless. How could the All-wise have created something without a purpose? We ourselves can determine the aim of our life, whether it shall be good or evil; we possess a free will, which can be used to shape our fate. The Qur'ān contains a sort of 'parable': the Almighty wished to entrust something to the heavens, the earth and the mountains, but they did not accept it and refused, fearing that they would not be capable of fulfilling the task. But man undertook to bear it (Chapter 33.72).

Under certain conditions a man is allowed by Islam to have more than one wife; the number is limited to four. Before the emergence of Islam the whole of Arabia was polygamous and had no legal or religious regulations concerning the treatment of women. Writers have often waxed sarcastic over the fact that after the death of his first wife Khadija, Muhammad had several wives at the same time. While Khadija lived Muhammad's marriage was purely monogamous, but afterwards he embarked on several marriages. Muhammad had lived unmarried until his twenty-fifth year, from his twenty-fifth to his fifty-fourth year he was married to one wife (Khadija), from his fifty-fourth to his sixtieth year he had more than one wife, and from then on until his death he contracted no more marriages. According to the British orientalist Muhammad Marmaduke Pickthall (who was converted to Islam and became well known for his translation of the Qur'ān), the concept of marriage as taught by Islam is completely different from the Western idea. There is no question of the 'union of two souls' or even of love. Every human being is lonely from the cradle to the grave, unless he finds the way to draw closer to Allah. Man is free and independent of every other human soul, he has his own responsibility (he is responsible for himself) and must bear his own burdens. In this respect there is no difference between man and woman. There is no fusion of two personalities in a Muslim marriage; each partner remains distinct. They have entered upon a union solely in order to fulfil certain duties towards each other. Marriage thus is not a sacrament, but rather a civil contract between the two 'free servants of Allah'. This does not mean that the marriage union cannot be sanctified by mutual love, but if this love is missing, the contract may be terminated. Divorce is possible; the man may at any time repudiate his wife by means of a fixed formula, but in this case the repudiated wife has the right to her dowry. She, too, can obtain a dissolution of the marriage if the man does not fulfil his marital duties, or she may buy her freedom by renouncing her right to the dowry. Polygamy, according to Pickthall (*Islamic Culture*), is not an Islamic institution, but merely a concession to human nature. The Qur'ān does not prescribe it, but recommends it in certain circumstances, whenever the alternative is to leave a woman helpless and without a defender. The fate of widows, for example, was originally extremely cheerless, and one of the reasons why Muhammad contracted more than one marriage was that he wished to give these widows, usually the wives of his friends who had fallen in war, a new safe status. These alliances were also intended to serve as a means of concluding treaties with neighbouring heads of tribes and other potentates. Of the women whom Muhammad married after the death of Khadija, the youthful Ayesha, daughter of Abu Bekr, his successor, was the only one whom he chose for her special qualities. He saw in her the woman who would be a perfect model for humanity.

The veiling of women is not directly advocated either by the Qur'ān or by the law. It originated in early Christian circles which stipulated that woman should adopt an attitude of reserve in the presence of men. She may show her face only in the family circle.

It will be necessary to dwell a little on the *hajj* (the annual pilgrimage to Mecca) which every Moslem is supposed to undertake once in his life, time and circumstances permitting. Much has been written – most of it critical – about the pilgrimages, which were formerly extremely hazardous from the hygienic point of view. These gatherings of many thousands of people repeatedly gave rise to terrible epidemics of plague, cholera, dysentery and typhus. The year 1893 was particularly disastrous when about 2,500 pilgrims died of cholera in a single day in Mecca. Countless hundreds never returned home from their pilgrimage. They fell victim not only to epidemics, but to the lamentable accommodation, the privations of the journey, exploitation by irresponsible enterprises, and sometimes, too, to attacks by bands of robbers. None the less the pilgrimage persisted through the centuries and participation has sharply increased during recent years with the development of communications.

Most pilgrims travel by sea to Jeddah where, after a ritual purification, they don the prescribed clothing, the *ihram*, consisting of two seamless white cloths, one to be draped around the upper part of the body and the other about the loins. Having arrived in Mecca the pilgrims first complete the ceremonial walk around the Kaaba. This is performed with the face turned towards the Black Stone in one of the walls of the Kaaba, in such a way that it is situated at the side where the human heart beats. This stone is said to have been brought to earth by one of the angels and placed in Mecca as the visible sign of God's existence. This circumambulation is repeated seven times. If the crowd is not too dense, the Black Stone may be kissed, or otherwise merely touched with the hand. It is even sufficient to point to it.

This, however, is still only the so-called little *hajj* or *oemrah*. The great *hajj*, the pilgrimage proper, is undertaken in the month of Dulheggia, the twelfth month of the Muslim year. It opens with the same walking round the Kaaba, after which all the pilgrims proceed to the plain of Arafat where they spend the entire day. No special ceremonies are prescribed. The night is spent in the little village of Moezdalifa, which is entirely uninhabited outside the *hajj* period. The day of festival falls on the tenth of Dulheggia. This is the Feast of Sacrifice, so-called on account of the sacrifices offered, not only by the pilgrims, but by all Muslims throughout the entire world. The Feast of Sacrifice comprises an impressive number of ceremonies, great and small; the meat of the sacrificial animals is distributed among the needy.

This is by no means the end of the *hajj*. According to the

regulations the crowd once again makes for Mecca, stoning the devil at the appropriate places on the way. The pilgrims' day is completely taken up with the various religious ceremonies. Before setting off again for their own countries the pilgrims keep three days of feasting, interrupted by a number of ritual ceremonies. Finally they scatter again to various parts of the world, weary and exhausted, with little money left, but happy in the consciousness that they have been pleasing to Allah and to his Prophet.

While in Mecca some of the pilgrims take the opportunity to make a subsidiary pilgrimage to Medina, the second Holy City of Islam which contains the tomb of the Prophet. This pilgrimage is not obligatory, but is often undertaken by Muslims from all parts of the world who, for their particular interests and desires, wish to obtain the intercession of the dead Prophet or of the Imams who are buried there. During the course of time many enterprising individuals have propagated the pilgrimage to Medina, not only from the religious, but also from the touristic standpoint. Sayings of Muhammad are dredged up from murky sources, including utterances in the following style: 'On the Day of Judgment I shall intercede for anyone who visits me either during my lifetime or after my death.' Even more drastically, he is supposed to have uttered the threat: 'On the Day of Judgment I shall punish everyone who goes on pilgrimage to Mecca and neglects to visit my tomb in Medina; but I shall act as intermediary for the believer who does visit my tomb, and my intervention will assure him of Paradise.'

Although many are accustomed to speak disparagingly of 'modern achievements' in the domain of culture and communications, it must be recognized that the modernizing of many localities and religious customs undertaken during the past few years by the Saudi-Arabian government has led to the disappearance of many former abuses. The exploitation of pilgrims is a thing of the past, and official tariffs have been drawn up so that travellers are no longer duped by get-rich-quick operators. The successive International Health Conferences, where the interested countries met in order to discuss measures to protect pilgrims against disease, have led to the drawing up of clearly stipulated international conventions. New, wide roads have been laid out; small shops, which struck a discordant note in the neighbourhood of the Kaaba, have been cleared away. The spacious design of the pilgrimage centre built not long ago makes it possible for half a million pilgrims at a time to attend the religious ceremonies.

In comparatively recent times a most remarkable pilgrim was the cause of considerable unrest. This was the celebrated Muhammad ibn Abdullah, called the 'Mad Mullah', an anti-English *mahdi* from British Somaliland who made a pilgrimage to Mecca in 1895 and returned with his authority among his tribesmen so enhanced that he united the Somalis in a new mystical order. He commanded a fanatical fighting force which time and again rose up successfully against British rule. English and Italian expeditions were sent to put down the danger-ous trouble maker. They succeeded in 1905 but a few years later he embarked upon guerilla activities which were only completely suppressed in 1920. The *mahdi* fled and died shortly afterwards in Ogaden.

For the non-Muslim, Mecca has always been a city of mystery, since he is denied entry to this sacred ground. Yet this has not prevented an increasing number of theologians, archaeologists, scholars and publicists from various parts of the world from penetrating Mecca, either in disguise or other-wise camouflaged, and contemplating the holy places.

Muhammad believed that he was destined to convey to his people the same message that the Old Testament prophets had brought to the Jews and that the Prophet Jesus had given to the Christians. He saw the world divided into peoples who all received one and the same message, differing only in language and according to the outward circumstances of the hearers.

It was three centuries before Islam developed into a world religion. It was disseminated and brought to the West in various forms, carried by scribes, by army commanders and by nomad tribes. Sometimes they fought each other in fanatical religious zeal, but usually they were united in a pan-Islamic movement which – to outsiders at least – seemed to aspire to the conquest of the world.

When one learns more of Islam one begins to recognize a religion which is in many respects related to both Christianity and Judaism. In all three the history of Revelation goes back to the same Father: Abraham, the founder of the Jewish people which sprang from his son Isaac, but also the founder of the Arabian people which sprang from his son Ishmael, born of the union between Abraham and Hagar, the slave of Sara. Ishmael, as firstborn, was according to the Arabic-Muslim idea the first rightful claimant. Ishmael's twelve sons became the founders of twelve Arabian tribes.

According to the late Professor Dr J. H. Kramers (*The World Religions*, ed. C. J. Bleeker), it is by no means certain that Muhammad himself was aware of having sown the seeds of a world religion. His aim was a religious attitude to life, characterized by the following of the precepts of the Qur'ān and the example given by himself as prophet with regard to ritual and other commandments. From the Qur'ān itself it appears that monotheistic ideas were already to some extent current in west Arabia before Muhammad transformed them into a religious doctrine. There are indications in the Qur'ān that even before Muhammad some individuals worshipped one God. These were called *hanifs* and there was a time when the word *haniffija* was used to refer to the doctrines later preached by Muhammad.

It has often been asked how it was possible that the Arabs, who until the seventh century remained entirely outside the circle of historic peoples, suddenly succeeded in founding an enormous and flourishing empire. How could these Arabs conquer the greater part of the Byzantine Empire, destroy the Visigothic Empire and become masters of Christian countries like Egypt and Africa, the homes of the greatest of the Church Fathers? Even the Holy Land, where Christ had dwelt and given his light to the world, fell to the supporters of Islam. And this well-nigh miraculous conquest was accomplished almost as much by the spirit as by the sword. The sword was mighty but the spirit was still mightier.

The time of Muhammad's first successor, Abu Bekr, who called himself Caliph Rasul Allah, meaning 'the Successor of Allah's Messenger' saw an enormous and violent expansion of those regions where Islam reigned. Abu Bekr succeeded in restoring the authority of Mecca's rule throughout the greater part of Arabia; his successor Omar, the second Caliph, extended the conquests in the direction of the mouth of the Tigris, and also towards Syria with the conquest of Damascus and Palestine. When he came to power, Mecca was waging full-scale war with Byzantium and Persia; his army consolidated the victories of his predecessor, and in 637 occupied Jerusalem, which now became a Muslim city. Having brought the whole of Mesopotamia into subjection, Omar's army marched on Egypt, which offered little resistance.

In the former Dutch East Indies a colony of Muslim merchants was found (in Perlak) in the thirteenth century. It was not, however, until around 1345 that Islam gained a firm foothold in the Archipelago – a Muslim sultan ruled on Sumatra, and Java had a *wali*, 'friend of God', Moelana Malik Ibrahim, as its first Islamic apostle. Along with Hinduism and Buddhism, which on Java, Sumatra, Borneo and Celebes had influenced the animistic philosophy of the Indonesians, Islam offered new perspectives and a new religious doctrine which were rapidly absorbed, first by the more educated section of the population, but later also by the less cultivated masses.

Meanwhile, outside Indonesia, terrible wars, internal disputes, murders and revolts accompanied the establishment of the Empire. Dynasties rose and fell. The entire Arabic world was convulsed, and the political power of the Muslim conquerors extended ever farther, in bloody battles across Asia, Africa and Europe, reaching a climax in 1580 when the Turks from Constantinople appeared before the gates of Vienna, presenting a direct menace to Christianity. The religion usually followed the political expansion. The centre of Islam as a world religion moved from Arabia to Damascus, and later to Baghdad and Cairo. By the beginning of the eleventh century Islam had developed from a simple moral doctrine and religion, as preached by Muhammad to a small community, into a complex of theological trends and sects and a hotch-potch of congregations, each with its own ritual and with an amazing diversity of religious concepts and practices. Yet there existed already the first visible signs of a trend which aimed at achiev-

ing union on the basis of religious and political unity. In Arabia
the motive power was Muhammad Ibn Abdul Wahab, who
waged war on all the superstitions and abuses which had gradually infiltrated the practice of the religion. His followers, the
Wahabites, however, went further than their leader had intended and took up arms against their neighbours. They conquered central and eastern Arabia, succeeded in entering Mecca
in 1806, purified the city and compelled it to accept a stern
asceticism. However, their political power was of short dura-
tion, although Wahabitism persisted. It was defeated in its turn
by the mighty Emir of the cities of Dariya and Riad, called
Mohammed ibn Saud. A life and death struggle raged between
various tribes and desert dwellers, accompanied by blood baths,
marauding expeditions and plunder. Ultimately Abdul Aziz,
son of one of the descendants of Mohammed ibn Saud, became
in our day the ruler of the large kingdom of Saudi Arabia. He
reigned as King Saud in the kingdom which he founded, where
eastern feudal conditions still persist and the slave trade is a
source of income. His son, Saud ibn Abdul Aziz, has established a closer link with the West, based on the country's oil
wealth.

This chapter might bear too much resemblance to a chronicle
or to a history book summary were we to follow too closely the
political expansion and decline of Islam. Islam has lost nothing
of its religious force, but its cultural impact has been considerably weakened by the rise of Western European culture. During
the nineteenth century extensive Muslim territories fell under
the political power of Western states, and their populations
were compelled to adapt their whole attitude to life to the
principles current in Western Europe which were in many
cases directly opposed to those of Islam. We know that until
the first World War Arabia was a Turkish province with the
Sultan of Constantinople as spiritual ruler. In the years pre-
ceding the war there were frequent revolts against the Sultan-
ate. In 1909 Sultan Abdul Hamid II was deposed by the young
Turks and the pan-Islamic idea transformed into a 'Greater
Turkish' ideal. During the 1914-18 war the entire Islamic world
was in ferment, and with the coming of peace new kingdoms

appeared, either independent or as mandated territories: Palestine, the Hejaz, Syria, Lebanon, Transjordan, Iraq. After the second World War Pakistan and Indonesia joined the independent Muslim states. This has had radical external political consequences, including the setting up of the Arab League which is so violently opposed to Zionism and the Republic of Israel.

In the political field, the unifying force which characterizes Islam has repeatedly failed to assert itself. There was nearly always a political background to the splits which have occurred in the course of time. However, despite the political differences which divide the Arab states, the Islamic religion has not lost its deep sense of unity and solidarity.

Through the centuries Islam has always been, from a theological point of view, a vital religion. This is revealed by the numerous sects, groups and dissident communities which grew up, based either upon aspirations towards modernism or dedicated to promoting a purer form of belief or a particular exegesis of the Qur'ān. There are, for example, the Kharijites (seceders) who call themselves the oldest Muslim sect, and the Shia, who derive their name from the Shi'at Ali (the party of Caliph Ali). The doctrine of the Shia is the official religion in present-day Iran (Persia), while in Iraq and northern India sections of the Muslim population are also Shia. There is in addition the sect of the Druses and also very many other groups each with its own doctrines which mostly concern only the interpretation of various minor points. Muhammad's original teaching remains inviolate.[1]

In the beginning there was considerable dispute about the interpretation of the Qur'ān. The extreme gnostic and dualistic interpretations, for example, were rejected as heresy. For two centuries the struggle against the Hellenistic interpretation advocated by the so-called School of Mutazilites occupied a central place in orthodox Islam. This school adopted the view-

---

[1] The Abbasids, descendants of Muhammad's uncle, Al Abbas, and the Fatimids, who descend from the prophet through his daughter Fatima, are family dynasties and represent no particular religious conviction.

B

point that grievous sinners ought not to be relegated to hell or be allowed to share in paradise, but occupy an intermediate position between belief and unbelief. According to other schools God must be seen as Infinite Justice, Infinite Power, Infinite Love and Grace; their opponents judged that the setting of limits to the power of God was an arbitrary concept, since these limits were expressed in terms which have their origin in human reason.

One of the most interesting movements is the Ahmadiyya sect, founded in 1880 by Mirza Ghulam Ahmad of Punjab. It is regarded by theologians as a heterodox movement which proclaims that Jesus was not crucified in Jerusalem but went to the East, where his tomb is to be found at Shrinagar in Kashmir. This Ghulam Ahmad claimed to be the reincarnation of Jesus and the Mahdi awaited by the Muslims. Comparatively recently (in 1914), this movement split into two groups. Both groups (the oldest has its headquarters in Rabwah, the more recent in Lahore) are frequently in the news through their missionary activities in Europe which have resulted in many Europeans being converted to Islam.

It is thought possible (indeed many Western theologians are convinced) that the spiritual trends in Islam originated under the influence of both Buddhism and Christianity. Along with the official Islam of the 'scribes' they have exercised considerable influence upon the mass of believers. For the Muslim mystic, the Sufi, the concepts of Beauty and God are identical. Sufism is seen as the esoteric side of Islam and flourished particularly in Persia. This Sufism cannot be identified with the modern Sufi movement which was introduced to Europe at the end of the last century by the Indian Inayat Khan. All the aspects of later Muslim mysticism, including the symbol of Light, are already latent in Islam and may be discerned in the Qur'ān.

According to the most recent statistics the Muslim world is now much more extensive than in the days of the political and cultural flowering of Islam. The total number of Muslims is reckoned to be around three-hundred to three-hundred-and-fifty million. They are scattered throughout Arabia, in the

Wahhabi kingdom of Saudi-Arabia, with the Hejaz, Mecca and Medina, in the Yemen, in the separate regions of Aden, Hadramut and Kuweit (Muslims of various tribes), and are also found in Tunisia, Algeria and Morocco, Libya, Tripolitania and Cyrenaica, West, East and Central Africa, Iraq, Iran, India, Pakistan, Turkey and in a number of the states which form part of the Union of Socialist Soviet Republics (Azerbaijan, Kazan, Turkoman, etc.). France alone has more than 80,000 Muslims and each of these sects and groups has its own history, its periods of growth and decline, its wars and peaceful development. The Islamic ideal, a universal Muslim state under one temporal head, was never realized, and in our modern world the pan-Islamic idea has lost much of its fanatical impetus. On the other hand, Christian culture and Western civilization have never proved strong enough to convert even one of the Muslim peoples to Christianity. What the many thousands of Asiatics who fought in the two World Wars saw at the front was in no way calculated to increase their understanding of, and admiration for, the civilized norms of the Western world.

Throughout the centuries, in periods of calm and stress, Muslim lawyers have worked to codify and set down the Muslim law, of which the doctrine of moral duties forms a part (see pp. 22-29). It indicates in the main which actions are obligatory, which are recommended, disapproved of or forbidden. The purely juridical concepts, as we know them, are only dealt with in certain contexts. Since 900 Muslim law is considered as definitely established for all time, based upon the four recognized schools of law: the Hanafite, Shafi-ite, Malakite and Hanbalite, called after four celebrated lawyers of the eighth and ninth centuries. The Shafi-ite school is followed in Indonesia and Malakka, along the coasts of Siam and India, in Hadramut, Western Arabia, Egypt, Syria and East Africa; the Hanafite in Turkey, Pakistan, Hindustan and Central Asia; the Malakite in Morocco, Tunisia and Algeria; the Hanbalite in Central Arabia and along the Persian Gulf. Professor Kramers called the Muslim law an ideal legal system which, however, is never applied in its entirety, since it was evolved more or less independently of social, political and economic circumstances. The Sacred Law is derived from certain sources, as desired by

Allah; it draws its authority exclusively from religion and has remained an integral part of the spiritual and religious culture.

As more modern legal concepts found their way into Muslim countries attempts were made to codify the Muslim law. Turkey was the first country to abandon the old system and replace it by a Western legal code. Other countries, including Egypt, followed her example, and Tunisia, since gaining her independence, seems inclined in this direction.

Muslim learning in the fields of philosophy, mathematics, physics, alchemy and medicine flourished early in Persia, Syria and Egypt, and in many respects laid the basis for the development of European learning. Until the end of the Middle Ages the Muslim peoples maintained a higher level of intellectual culture than that of the Christian lands. For years Baghdad was a centre of learning where works by the Greek masters on philosophy, medicine, mathematics and astronomy were translated into Arabic and which produced important scientific works by Muslim scholars. These inspired numerous European scholars of the twelfth century to travel to Spain in order to learn enough Arabic to read these works in the original.

Islamic art, which fluctuates considerably, is still today an inexhaustible source of study. It is closely connected with the religious life, contains many non-Arabic elements and is essentially a decorative art which finds expression in the adornment of the mosques. Although the Qur'ān does not expressly forbid the depiction of living beings, most Muslim artists consider this an unwritten law. Not all, however; artists in Persia have never paid any attention to it.

Although a specifically Islamic or Muslim art only emerged in the seventh century, it is based upon the Arabic style which it has been possible to reconstruct with a considerable degree of accuracy from the numerous excavations and archaeological finds. Mosque architecture especially has had periods of great brilliance. A mosque, however, cannot be compared altogether with a church. The name mosque merely refers to the place where one prostrates oneself as a sign of subjection to Allah. In actual fact the mosque is the walled space in which the ceremony is performed under the open sky. Since the faithful kneel in rows in a mosque, and must have room to bow down, the mosque contains no seats or other furniture except the *minbar* (pulpit), a sort of little tower with a staircase attached. The exterior of the mosque may differ considerably from country to country, but inside they must all meet the same requirements.

Decorative palaces and houses richly ornamented with arabesques and fretwork still testify to the past glory of true craftmanship. Weaving, wickerwork and pottery objects were the principal expressions of art and craftwork produced by craftsmen who understood their craft, loved their work and were not simply out to make money.

Both art and learning owe much to Caliph Al Mansur (754-775) who had to wade through rivers of blood before he succeeded in establishing his dynasty, that of the Abbasids. It was he who founded the new capital Baghdad ('given by God'), one of the most splendid cities of the Middle Ages. It was during Al Mansur's reign that the basis was laid for the study of the Arabic language, from which developed the literary works which have enriched world literature.

There were no poets or writers during the wars of conquest immediately following the death of Muhammad, or if there were, they remained silent. Yet already during the rule of the Umayyads a religious school of poetry developed which was destined to become classic. The old Arabic writings provided the source of inspiration for Muslim literature, which in its turn produced young poets among those peoples which had become converted to Islam: Syrians, Mesopotamians, Egyptians. Arabic developed from the primitive Bedouin language and was for a long time the vehicle of a considerable world literature.

In his *Histoire de la Littérature Arabe*, published in 1943, the French speaking Muslim publicist Abd el Jalil gives a survey of Arabic religious-scientific writings, works of history (the Chronicles of the Crusades), geographical treatises, heroic epics, love poetry, novels and popular literature. One of the most famous works in this category is the celebrated *Thousand and One Nights (Alf laila wa-laila)*, the collection of stories and marvellous tales garnered at various times and in different countries and collected into one book. Life at the courts of the Muslim caliphs of Baghdad, like Haroun al Rashid, pro-

vided material for the tales of Princess Sheherazade, daughter
of the Grand Vizier of King Shahriar, who told the king a
different story each night for a thousand and one nights, thus
postponing each time the execution with which she was threatened. These stories find less favour among Muslims than in the
West. They are considered as inferior popular literature, and
Muslims wonder why the Western reader finds them so fascinating.

Turning to Muslim philosophy, it is derived from that of the
Greek philosophers, adapted to Islam. It dates only from the
middle of the eighth century, being based upon an adaptation
of Neo-platonic philosophical doctrines by the Arab philosopher Al-Kindi. He was followed by thinkers like Al-Faran
and Al-Razi who were the first representatives of a purely Arab
philosophy. In the eleventh century the centre of philosophical
activities moved to Persia, where the Iranian philosopher and
physician Al Hussein ibn Abdullah ibn Sina (called Avicenna
in the Latin translations of his works) constructed a new
system of logic. He found many supporters but even more
opponents including the Church Father Alghazali. It was not
until the twelfth century that Christian scholars in Spain translated the Muslim works into Latin so that Muslim philosophy
became widely known in the West.

Dr A. Th. Van Leeuwen has outlined the Muslim criticism of
Western culture: 'The internal crisis of the west, which already
makes it difficult for the westerner himself to gain any insight
into the deeper-lying order of his culture, acts as a barrier to a
truly intellectual confrontation with inhabitants of other cul-
tures, especially where penetration is experienced as imperial-
ism.' In his opinion conflict with the Western civilization is for
Islam 'unavoidably a confrontation with her hostile brother,
Christianity, against whom she has had to defend herself from
the hour of her birth. Whereas in the Middle Ages this confrontation was an unstable balance of power between two
religions of equal merit, new components have been added in
modern times by the totally changed position of Christianity
in relation to culture and society, the one-sided ascendancy of
the west and the dawning consciousness of Islam. The almost

exclusively dogmatic polemics and apologetics of the Medieval discussion have faded into the background, while now the argumentation resembles a guerilla-type war of movements over a wide political, social, economic and cultural front.'

According to Sir Hamilton Alexander Rosskeen Gibb (*Mohammedanism. An Historical Survey*, 1949), the dangers to which Islam, as a religion, is exposed are now greater than ever. The most obvious emanate from those forces which have undermined or threaten to undermine all theistic religions. The external pressure of secularism, whether in the deceptive form of nationalism or in the tenets of scientific materialism and the economic interpretation of history, have, in Gibb's view, already left their mark on various aspects of Muslim life. Yet even this influence, treacherous as it is, is probably in the long run less dangerous than the decline of the religious sense and the weakening of the ecclesiastical traditions of Islam.

It may well be that the reinterpretation of Islam in an effort to make of it an ideology attractive for modern times – garnished with a choice of Qur'ān texts and Tradition – has watered it down and weakened its theological content. It is, however, characteristic that despite political differences Islam has not lost her sense of community, the feeling that society must be preserved. Tolerance within Islam is one of her fundamental concepts, although she has frequently used force against outsiders. Yet is not Christianity, too, a religion of non-violence, which believes in the all-conquering power of love? And how often have those who profess it, failed to abide by their principles!

SUGGESTIONS FOR FURTHER READING

Rodwell, J. M., *The Koran*, Everyman

Dermenghem, E., *Muhammad*, Longmans

Gibb, H. A. R., *Mohammedanism, A Historical Survey*, 2nd ed., Oxford

Guillaume, A., *Islam*, Penguin

Mahmud, S. F., *The Story of Islam*, Oxford

Watt, W. M., *Muhammad, Prophet and Statesman*, Oxford

2

BRAHMANISM AND HINDUISM

IN ATTEMPTING to penetrate the mysteries and secrets of Brahmanism and Hinduism one must take care lest one lose one's way among the countless paths of mysticism, ethics, dogmatics and religious cults along which this Indian religious philosophy has wandered in the course of the centuries. We must abstain from any attempt at scientific interpretations or those of comparative religion, but merely seek simple words with which to explain the origin of these philosophies, their content, development and socio-religious aspects.

Brahma, a Sanskrit word, originally referred not to a divinity but to an invisible force which priests attributed to their songs and proverbs in order to strengthen the gods and render them favourably inclined towards humanity. There was admittedly the Brahmanaspati or Brahspati, the 'Lord of Prayer', the divine priest with magical powers who embodied 'the neuter' Brahma. In the course of time Brahma came to be viewed more as a divine substance, the Head of the Universe, the One Eternal, and Brahspati was transformed into Brahma. Those priests who had acquired the knowledge of the Brahma were called Brahmins, and Brahma represented the impersonal force, beyond good and evil, representing the original principle of all things. He was not, however, completely unpersonified, for the masses regarded him as placed above the other gods, the creator of the world and the inspirer of the Vedas. Together with Shiva ('Great God', 'gracious one') and Vishnu, one of the chief gods whose form resembles that of a sun god, Brahma composed the so-called *Trimurti* (Trinity), dwelling in his own heaven, the *Brahmaloka*, and depicted as having four heads and four arms, seated upon a lotus blossom or a swan. He also had a consort called *Sarasvati*. The sacred river which rises in the western part of Tibet and has a length of nearly 375 miles was given the name Brahmaputra or 'Son of Brahma', since this is how the Indians regarded it.

As we have already mentioned, Brahma is said to have inspired the Vedas, the immense and extremely ancient collection of precepts, rites, sacred texts, proverbs and hymns of magical import. There are four collections of Vedas: the *Rig Veda* ('Veda of Praise', hymns of preponderantly mythical content), the *Sama Veda* (the Veda of the songs), the *Yajur Veda* (proverbs for the great sacrifices and for the simple sacra) and finally the *Atharva Veda* which, more than the first three, is complete in itself. This main classification can again be subdivided into: Samhitas (the collection of the respective texts), Brahmanas (dissertations on the meaning and aim of the rites and formulae), Aranykas (an explanation of the secret rites), Upanishads (the 'secret teaching', the conclusion of the Vedas, which are generally thought to have originated between 100 and 500 B.C.) and the *sutras* (literally strings, guidelines, i.e. guidelines to the ritual). The *Rig Veda* is the most important of the Vedas. It is a collection of 1,028 hymns each of about ten verses. Together with the Avesta, it forms the earliest documents of the Indo-Germanic peoples. The aim of Vedas (meaning knowledge) is the obtaining of what one desires and the avoidance of what one does not desire. Later it acquires the more metaphysically orientated meaning of that redeeming knowledge which liberates from suffering in this world.

Originally, the study of the Vedas and the performing of the sacral actions described therein was reserved exclusively for the three highest castes: the Brahmins or priestly caste, the kings and nobility, and the third caste, the merchant, what we would call the well-to-do middle class. The fourth caste – the *Shudra* or servile class – was not allowed to participate. This brings us to one of the most desperate problems of Indian society, the caste system. We shall have more to say of it later.

The Brahmins thus form the highest caste in Indian society. Not all Brahmins are priests; they also include scholars and teachers who are entitled to conduct the religious ceremonies and sacrificial offerings among the Aryans, the members of the highest castes. The principal characteristics in the last stage are beliefs in a super-divine power, in transmigration and in reincarnation. According to this last doctrine every being at death passes from one existence to another as determined by the *karma*, the sum of the good and evil deeds in the existence just completed. A new existence awaits every dying being: whether it be as divinity, person, animal or inmate of hell is decided by the person's merits. Just as in Buddhism, one has the cycle of existences from which it is possible to escape through introspection and self-denial. We shall deal more fully with this idea in our chapter on Buddhism.

The vedic rites with relation to birth, marriage and death are colourful, profound and moving. They are motivated by a kind of fear, a fear of dangers which must be averted. The young woman's impregnation, her pregnancy, the birth of her child, are accompanied by certain rites which are intended to fortify her as she enters upon each new stage of her life. The marriage ceremony comprises an almost endless series of meaningful ceremonies, all of which are intended to prevent disasters, to conquer superstition and to open the way to prosperity. In his study on Brahmanism and Hinduism the late Professor B. Faddegon writes of the sacrament of the disposal of the dead, which reveals the great fear of ritual impurity: 'The close relatives of the deceased man eat only food which they have bought or have been given, since food from the house of mourning is contaminated. They are not allowed contact with anything holy which means, for example, that they may not study the Veda.' The head of a family had to be cremated with his own hearth fire. The person thus ritually cremated, it was thought, entered upon a new existence, and for this reason was always dressed in new garments. On the third or tenth day the bones were collected, purified, placed in an urn and buried. They might then possibly be dug up again much later and re-interred elsewhere, at a spot with many plants, under a burial mound. Seeds were sown upon this mound to provide food for the deceased. The custom also existed of cremating with the deceased various objects which might prove useful to him in the after life. More important, in the opinion of Professor Faddegon, than all the symbolic idea-associations, is the fact that the believer accepts them all, however contradictory, as the expression of one fundamental reality. 'It may be said that beneath the conscious belief in any particular symbolic representation, lives the deeper, subconscious belief in death as the unavoidable consequence and inherent condition of all life.'

Any attempt to explain the extremely complicated system of offering would require a thorough knowledge of Hindu theology and mythology quite beyond our competence and also beyond the scope of this outline. We shall content ourselves with mentioning the distinction between the full and new moon sacrifices which consist of a long series of actions, symbolic duties and recitations. Among the numerous gods to whom sacrifice is made we meet familiar names like that of Agni, the god of Fire and mediator in the sacrifice between gods and men, Indra, the god of War or God-warrior-and-conqueror, and Soma, the great godhead, king of plants and waters, who fortifies the gods in their struggle against the forces of evil. 'He safeguards against death and his worshippers attain to an eternal world of light.'

Brahmanism and Hinduism can be said to have merged. Hinduism, which originated around the beginning of the Christian era, is usually considered as the third phase in the evolution of Brahmanism, the fusion of an entire complex of religions, races and social institutions, or rather of a multiplicity of religions which closely resemble each other and are attuned to each other. The proliferation of sects makes it difficult even for the Indians themselves to pick out characteristics valid for them all. They do, however, possess some doctrines in common: the transmigration of souls, an aspiring to be freed from the cycle of rebirths, a recognition of the *karma* and Brahma. They also cling to the authority of the Vedas and to the dogma of rebirth, which holds out to everyone the promise of more lives in which to attain to a higher plane.

In the West, Hinduism is almost always defined as the socio-religious aspect of the Indian culture of the last two thousand years. There is an astonishing diversity in the manner in which gods or higher powers are venerated. Hinduism embraces not only fetishism, ritual strangulation and a belief in demons but also lofty philosophical systems, unconditional submission to

one personal god and a stern asceticism. Hindus themselves
would deny any accusation of pantheism. God, the eternal, pri-
maeval being, Brahma who reveals himself, is in *everything*,
every man, every plant, every animal, every stone, and each
must honour him in the manner he thinks best. There are also,
however, other divinities which are not eternal and which are
venerated in the most diverse fashions. Hinduism thus has no
founder whose teachings form the basis of its doctrine, nor is
there any hierarchy. There is no beginning, Hinduism is eternal.

What criteria then can be advanced to cover the concept
Hinduism? In his book on Hinduism, published in 1943, Professor J. Gonda has succeeded in giving a comprehensive
list of the main tenets of Hinduism. He names first of all a
belief in an absolute and all-embracing principle, the only real
and true principle, the Brahma. Brahma is ceaselessly active in
the world, creating, preserving, changing, and in these aspects
forms a trinity of three great gods: Brahma, Vishnu and Shiva.
Next is the recognition of the Vedas and of the supremacy of
the Brahmin caste, to which is entrusted the study of the Vedas
and the performance of religious ritual. Then come the practice
of vegetarianism (the cow is a sacred animal), the belief in the
dogma of rebirth and a striving towards freedom from the
necessity of being born again. This idea of redemption occupies
a central place not only in Hinduism but also in Buddhism and
in Jainism, the religious-philosophical sect of India which
originated at the same time as Buddhism as a reaction against
the supremacy of the Brahmin caste.

Every Hindu feels himself bound to his surroundings, to the
past and to the universe by the concept of Dharma, the fundamental concept in life and teaching, the sum total of qualities
inherent in any person or thing by virtue of his or its nature.
'Dharma is law, regularity, harmony, the norm prevailing in
the world of nature and man', and each has the task of ac-
complishing his part in the eternal and universal Dharma. To
keep the established customs of one's family, caste, sex, office
and age is to live according to the Dharma. Not to observe the
Dharma (called Adharma) does not mean to sin, but implies the
disturbance of harmony and balance. There is a textbook of
the Dharma, the *Dharmashastra*, which is not a code of law but

merely sets out and explains what is pure and what is impure. The idea of pure and impure is based on a belief in an infinite number of powers and forces which can work for good or evil. Those who act wrongly meet a bad end both in this world and after death. To say that a thing is pure means that it is free of magical or religious dangers. When eating, care must be taken that no evil spirits enter the mouth with the food; the destruction of trees, necessary to man for his food, brings danger. The dead and outcasts can contaminate; lies and slander are a danger to anyone guilty of them. It is better to avoid any contact with strangers, since they do not follow the Dharma. It is therefore undesirable to learn a foreign language.

Most Westerners cannot help but think that the religion of the Indian is little more than primitive. For the most part fear predominates, and the number of inferior divine and demoniac powers runs into thousands. Every possible source of good or evil is venerated or feared. Places where special events have taken place, whether for good or for evil, are approached with awe, even tools are treated with reverence, and numerous tribes have their own particular 'village gods'. Professor Gonda writes: 'Village gods are usually feminine, whereas the higher Hindu pantheon contains a majority of male figures. They have only slightly differentiated and vaguely defined functions and a limited sphere of influence (to avoid their wrath it is sufficient to move house). Animal sacrifices are made to them, which is in conflict with Brahmanistic ideas. Usually they inspire only fear, are not venerated with loving submission and have at most a small sanctuary: sometimes none at all. Their priests are not Brahmins but persons of differing castes and callings. Their cult and existence does not give rise to dogmas or philosophical theories. The cholera and smallpox goddesses are greatly feared; amulets are worn or lights burned as protection against them, and attempts are made to drive them away with noise and exorcism rites. The idea of the scapegoat is also known: a pig is bought from the communal funds, the "contamination" is heaped upon it and it is then driven into the wilderness.' Those demons which bring misfortune and sickness can assume various shapes; they dwell in the wilderness and some of them are merely the souls of the dead. Snakes are feared, trees vener-

ated, water not only purifies physically but also banishes the
evil (the causes of evil). Many old people or those incurably ill
make their way to the Ganges, one of the seven holy rivers, in
order to die there and so leave this life in a state of purity.
Special honour is paid to the forces of fertility; in spring gifts
are brought to *Kama*, the god of sexual love. These spring
festivities are the occasion for physical excesses which are
intended to promote fertility.

Although to satisfy the desire for sensual pleasure is considered as the lowest aim in life, joy obtained through the senses
is for the Hindu a necessary requirement for the proper development of the body. Lack of it can lead to sadness, melancholy and despair. Like all the occupations of day-to-day
existence the exercise of the sexual act may not be left to blind
instinct. It must be learnt, and its aims, conditions and methods
must be defined theoretically lest it become intolerable. Brahma
already proclaimed the *ars amatoria*, and numerous Indian
writers have occupied themselves in setting down the ways in
which physical intercourse may take place. In the third century
A.D. Vatsayana – a most estimable man – wrote his celebrated
work the *Khama Sutra*, which enjoys a doubtful reputation in
the West. Undeservedly so, for in Indian literature it is considered a classic and to this very day is held by the Hindu to
contain the religious exposition of the art of love. It was in fact
Vatsayana's intention to inspire restraint (austerity) in the
enjoyment of love since in the final analysis it brings only
sorrow.

None the less some remarkable manifestations of eroticism
are found among some of the sects. Professor Faddegon mentions members of certain monastic communities who dress in
women's clothes and even practise an inner travesty. Other,
clearly masochistic traits among the monks were the custom of
eating from a skull (expressing a warlike and vengeful spirit
with the skull representing the enemy's head), the carrying of a
club to symbolize the masculine instincts, the possession of
physical and bellicose passions, and the smearing of the body
with the ashes of cremated corpses as an expression of self-
abasement.

Hinduism can be described as an extremely varied cult, characterized on the one hand by a profound symbolism, on the other by primitive fear and unbridled physical passions. Self-torture, penitential exercises and absolute humiliation are its principal characteristics. These imply at the same time that social realities are avoided, that life is held cheap, and that rites are practised which are accepted among the masses from generation to generation. They are not, however, practised by all, for among the higher classes of Hindu society many have abandoned these psychologically orientated religious practices.

From the diversity of the Hindu pantheon we shall briefly examine the two 'highest gods', Shiva and Vishnu. Brahma is admittedly the 'all Highest', but he is thought of impersonally and he possesses no characteristics. Shiva, on the other hand, represents cosmic forces such as production and destruction; he is more a force than a creating god. He is awe-inspiring; he dwells on the Himalaya and is distinguished for his blood lust and destructive urge. He tarries on the battlefields and decks himself out with skulls and bones. His mouth is frightful, his red, terrifying figure bestial. He is followed by a wicked dog, and his influence is destructive, although he is also capable of good deeds if he can be placated.

Alongside the male Shiva we have his female counterpart Shakti, who possesses the potential creative power that Shiva's activity renders possible. The sect named after her, the Shaktis, hold the opinion that the evil passions which dominate our world can be purified by an established love ritual which transforms the sacral pleasure of love into a mystical act leading to absorption in the universe. Shaktism, which is most widespread in Bengal, comprises a number of magical sacral formulas, the five *mantras*, which are considered as 'concentrated divine energy'. The Hindu who has progressed so far along the road to redemption as to achieve complete self-control is thought fitted to do that which is forbidden to other Hindus, e.g. *madya*, to drink intoxicating spirits, *mamsa*, to eat meat, *matsya*, to eat fish, *mudra*, to eat roasted grain and *maithuna*, to perform the sexual act. He carries out these acts with a pure heart, without desire; he has attained perfection; living, he is redeemed.

However, this idea of purity and redemption does not prevail everywhere. In many places the Shaktistic ritual, contaminated by the impure notions of unbalanced minds, has degenerated into orgies at which even human sacrifices are offered.

How refreshing, by contrast, is the figure of Vishnu, a youth wearing a jewel on his breast and a diadem upon his head and bearing in his *four* arms a discus, a shell, a cudgel and a lotus. He is seated upon a lotus leaf or upon the bird Garuda and intends only good. The layman is often repelled when contemplating an image of a Hindu divinity by the fact that the figure depicted possesses a greater number of limbs than is normal in a human being. One should, however, make the effort to overlook this, to the Western mind, incomprehensible superfluity, and to realize that the apparently excessive number of limbs is considered necessary by the artist for the holding and using of various attributes essential to the carrying out of the religious and magical acts and ceremonies.

Hinduism contains an inexhaustible wealth of mythological, magical and religious concepts and ideas. The most horrid fantasies alternate with delicate images, cruelty and gentleness go hand in hand. Each movement, each sect, possesses different forms, all of which aspire to restrain the destructive powers of the gods, to share in their forgiveness and peace, to gain communication with them and, by mortifying physical desires, studying the text of the Vedas and practising meditation, to achieve a higher state of consciousness.

The method most familiar in the West is *yoga*, the attempt to find the pure self or godhead through physical and mental concentration. To this end a series of very heavy obligations must be observed. *Yoga* is practised by many in the West as a physical exercise aimed at acquiring self-discipline in order consciously to make the body perfect and thus receptive to spiritual forces. This is the so-called *hatha-yoga*, a phrase somewhat obscurely explained in the book *Yoga and Health* by Selva Raja Yesudian and Elisabeth Haich. 'Our body is enlivened by positive and negative currents and when these currents are in complete equilibrium we enjoy perfect health. In the ancient language of the Orient, the positive current is designated by the letter "HA" which is equivalent in meaning to "SUN". The negative current is called "THA" meaning "moon". The word "yoga" has a double meaning. On the one hand, it is equivalent to "joining", while the second meaning is "yoke". The "Hatha yoga" signifies the perfect knowledge of the two energies, the positive sun and negative moon energies, their joining in perfect harmony and complete equilibrium and the ability to control their energies absolutely, that is, to bend them under the yoke of the "self".'

Hatha-yoga, in effect, carries us back to nature, familiarizes us with our own body and with the forces at work in the body, and leads us to an inner harmony of body and soul. The yogi is convinced that the origin of every illness lies in the soul. The self is essentially radiant, spotlessly pure and without sin. When, however, it veiled itself in matter and put on a body, it took upon itself the sin of matter, of the world. Matter, the subjection to time, limited its consciousness of self, and a million years' development were necessary before it again became conscious of itself in the body. Even today this development has not yet been completed since the consciousness of self of the average person has still far to go before it attains full freedom and union with his higher, divine, Self. The aim of *yoga* is, as defined, to render human consciousness dependent on our will, to broaden it deliberately and systematically and thus step by step to heighten and to steel the resistance of the bearer of the constantly increasing life energy – the nervous system. The ultimate aim is divine consciousness of self developed to perfection and its complete revelation in the body: the God-man. The Hindus call those who have attained the stage of perfection *Jiwan Mukta*.

The exercises of *hatha-yoga* are divided into three: control of the mind, control of breathing and control of the various positions of the body. They must be practised together; none of them is conceivable without the other two. They comprise numerous breathing exercises and positions of the body, which all have a name and purpose. In this connection we may refer to *mazdaznan* which, through the practice of a certain method of breathing, through song and prayer, aims at freeing the soul from the oppressive bonds of a not yet perfectly working body which seeks perfect health. *Mazdaznan*, which was only introduced to the West in its present form in 1901, i.e. as a physical cult founded on a religious cult, is associated with the religious movement, Mazdaism, founded in the fourth century B.C. by Zoroaster or Zarathushtra.

The origin of the caste system is difficult to determine. Essentially it has a religious basis, yet it may also be viewed as a sort of social grouping comprising trade organizations or guilds which, as in Western countries, developed into social classes. For the Indian who clings to tradition, the caste system is irrevocably linked with the *karma*. For him, belonging to a certain caste, whether it be that of the Brahmins (priestly caste), the so-called *Kshatriyas* (the nobility), the *Vaishyas* (farmers, merchants and manual workers) or the *Dasyus* and *Shudras* (the despised servant class) is a result of the experience, wisdom and spiritual culture acquired in previous existences. If one belongs to a lower caste he must regard this as his own fault since he evidently has failed to acquire sufficient wisdom in a previous existence. Until recently there were about 2,500 castes, though not all of them were represented in every part of India.

The inhuman status and way of life of the Untouchables were completely unthinkable in our Western society. There is no comparison even with the racial discrimination in some parts of the United States or the apartheid policy in South Africa. The Untouchables were shunned and avoided like lepers; a member of a higher caste felt impure after contact with an Untouchable, if the former accepted water or cooked food from an Untouchable he was removed from his caste. In fact, members of different castes never ate together since they feared the sin of contamination by a member of a lower caste. A member of a higher caste considered himself so tainted by even the shadow of an Untouchable that he could only purify himself from such contamination by bathing in holy water and doing stern penance.

All public institutions were prohibited to the outcasts, their children were not allowed to attend the public schools, in the villages they were not even allowed to draw water from the communal well. They were forbidden to cross the threshold of the Hindu temples, and no Brahmin was ever willing to perform the prescribed ceremonies at their marriages and burials.

The servants of the higher castes performed no services for the casteless, even though they themselves were Untouchables. The casteless were thus obliged to maintain their own priests and workers.

It is a tragic fact that certain groups of workers were excluded from normal human society by reason of their supposed ritual impurity. These included the tanners, who were held in great contempt by orthodox Hindus because they processed the skins of the sacred cows, the knackers, the street cleaners and sewer workers. Musicians, too, who played upon the drum, were also counted among the Untouchables. The mass of these, however, was formed by the millions of agricultural labourers who populated the villages and had for centuries by their hard labour helped the Indian princes to accumulate their vast fortunes.

The close connection which exists in Hinduism between religious ideas and social customs has led to a great number of abuses in the social field, which had acquired a supposed sanction through religious notions, being stubbornly defended by the orthodox. The most progressive among the religious leaders have not succeeded in eradicating these abuses entirely, or where they did, it was only within the narrow circle of their supporters who then formed another distinctive sect. Among the most horrible of these abuses were child-marriages and the treatment of widows. There was a time when a girl of eight, even of four or five, could be given in marriage, even though she remained in her parents' house until puberty. This custom, which has so frequently been condemned, originated from the Brahman doctrine which said that a mature girl who remained with her parents unmarried caused her father to descend to the deepest depths of sin, since he was guilty of the death of the children she might have borne. In 1891 the British administration brought in the Age of Consent Act, which set the marriageable age of girls at twelve. An attempt was also made to avoid child marriages by refusing to accept married boys as pupils in schools.

At one time a woman was permitted to marry only once. If she became a widow she was expected to remain in this state for the rest of her life, unless she allowed herself to be cremated with her husband, thus heightening the prestige of herself and her family. The decision was voluntary, but it had not always been so. In days long ago the widow of the deceased was flung into the fire with him 'because he needed her in the after life'. This custom was prohibited by British law in 1829, but this did not prevent many devoted wives from accompanying their spouses into the hereafter of their own free will. The ban on remarriage was also pernicious since many widows were still children when they were married off and were thus compelled to spend a lifetime alone after their husband's death. The British government also took measures to combat this injustice under pressure from enlightened Indian reformers. A law passed in 1856 declared a second marriage valid. Since this time the emancipation of the Indian woman has progressed rapidly and her position now can be compared with that of women in the West.

One could be temporarily excluded from one's caste for scrupulously defined transgressions, or even permanently excluded for the murder of a Hindu. Membership of a caste, however, did not imply any particular religious belief. One could, for example, become a Christian and still retain one's caste membership.

The fate of the Untouchables has been frequently described, and it cannot be said that no one took up their cause. Gandhi was one of their most ardent champions; he called them not Untouchables but *Harijans*, 'God's Elect'. On one of his visits to Delhi he lodged, by way of demonstration, in the street-cleaners' and refuse-collectors' quarter. These formed the lowest group of the Untouchables yet still observed a sort of class distinction among themselves. In this way Gandhi obliged all the high-caste Hindus who wished to meet him to enter the 'ghetto' of the Untouchables which up till now they had fearfully avoided.

We have spoken repeatedly of the Veda (knowledge), which refers to the whole of Indian literature in so far as it has been inwardly contemplated and intuitively experienced by inspired seers. Another name for this literature, to which is attributed the highest religious authority, is Sruti (knowledge through revelation) as compared with Smriti (knowledge through tradition) which is of course less authoritative. An almost perfect mastery of the subject would be required to deal with it in any way comprehensively and in order to attempt such a task we should soon be obliged to draw upon the works of those who have enriched our knowledge by their study of the Indian religions.

The various trends and philosophical systems of Hinduism, with their rituals and ceremonies, texts, magic formulae, sacral rules, verses, hymns and precepts are mazes in which it is pleasant to wander, even if the exit is not always easy to find. The number of different outlooks on life and on the world represented by the various sects is impressive. Hinduism has indeed been characterized as a 'collective idea' for the most divergent religious convictions, mythological and philosophical concepts and cults, which are often only loosely connected despite their common fundamental characteristics. In keeping with the tolerant mentality of the Hindu, the relationship between the various sects is usually friendly.

The existing orthodox sects are divided into four groups: the Vaishnavas who worship Vishnu as the supreme God; the Awas, for whom Shiva is the highest deity; the Shaktis, who venerate the female principle before all; the worshippers of Skanda, Surija and other gods (these are of little influence now). There are in addition sects which flatly deny the supernatural origin and the authority of the Vedas. They recognize only what can be perceived by the senses and do not believe in the existence of a 'soul', *Karma*, in the hereafter or in redemption. A remarkable phenomenon in our day is the rise of the Vaishesika, a school which proclaims that the world originated from atoms and explains its development from the viewpoint of the natural sciences. One important school, which came into prominence around A.D. 600, is Tantrism, which derives its name from the *Tantras*, writings which contain the teaching and rites. They comprise a sacral magic, based on the conviction that all objects of the universe are potentially present in Brahma and that certain magic rites enable man to attain supreme insight and domination over the transcendental powers.

All these sects produced great thinkers, including the Brahmins Madhva, Nimbarka and Shankara and the southern Indian Brahmin Ramanuja who lived in the eleventh century A.D. In the fourteenth century Ramanuja's follower, Ramananda, enjoyed considerable esteem in Benares. His work had a purifying effect and his stern morality did away with much of the eroticism which characterized other schools.

Hinduism, which embraced many forms of worship from other trends of thought but absorbed them into her own doctrine and way of thinking, produced poets whose lyric and epic works will live for ever. These included revolutionary poets who wove new ideas into the legendary fabric of their verses. Many of the later poets especially rejected the caste system and spoke out eloquently against polytheism and idolatry. There is a rather charming legend which concerns the poet Kabiro. In the fifteenth century there lived in the city of Benares a Brahmin widow who had a son. Evidently she felt unable to care for him, for she laid him in a basket and placed the basket upon the rippling waters of a lake filled with lotuses (now the sacred flower of the Buddhists), an act which recalls to mind the fate of Moses in the bullrushes on the banks of the Nile as described in Ex. 2.1-10. A Muslim weaver called Niru found the infant, took it home, consulted with his wife Nima, and together they decided to rear the child whom they called Kabir. As a boy Kabir learned the weaver's trade, but his interest lay more in religious questions. He studied the teaching of the poet Ramananda who said that there is only one God, that Truth is the greatest friend of humanity and that only a sober life can lead to nirvana, the end of the cycle of rebirths and the state of absolute bliss.

Kabir married and became a good husband and a good father to his two children. And as he sat all day at his loom, his spirit soared. In the evenings he wrote down his poetical thoughts on the meaning of life and the path that leads to God. He wrote in flowing verses which were eagerly read in Benares. He gained renown as a poet but continued to earn his living as a weaver. In his poems he incorporated the teachings of monotheism, combated the worship of idols and rejected the caste system. The number of his followers rapidly increased, and when he died at the age of seventy-nine both Brahmins and Muslims claimed him. The Brahmins said that Kabir had belonged to them because he was born a Brahman, the Muslims numbered him among their own because he had been brought up as a Muslim. The legend goes on to say that when his followers approached the corpse and raised the shroud they found, instead of his body, a wreath of flowers. His disciples collected his poems and sayings in a 'holy book' and called themselves *Kabir panthis*, the disciples of Kabir. There are about a million members of this sect in India at the present day.

One of the most important of the Hindu teachers who were strongly influenced by Islam was Baba Nanak, the 'glorious Nanak'. He endeavoured to reconcile Islam and Hinduism and to bring them to evolve interdependently. Nanak was the son of a prominent Hindu from Talwandi in the province of Lahore. Even as a boy he mastered Persian and Arabic and was preoccupied with religious problems. This, however, was not conducive to work, and no matter how his father insisted that he should learn a trade or occupy some position, Nanak continued to neglect his duties and spent his time reading the poems of Ramananda and Kabir. He was thirty years old when he decided to become a *Guru*, master (teacher), in a 'new' religion. This religion concentrated upon one God, Hari, the Creator whose grace is boundless and in whose presence man is powerless. Nanak gained many followers, broke with various Brahmin rites and drew up a temple service based on Muslim ritual. He journeyed through India to Ceylon, visited Kashmir and reached Arabia, where he preached his doctrine. His followers were called the Sikhs (disciples). At his death he was succeeded by another Guru, Arian, who collected Nanak's sayings and sermons. This leadership by one man eventually became hereditary, and under the sixth Guru Har Govind acquired a military and political character. In the eighteenth century the Sikhs waged war against the Muslim Mogul rulers from India. They founded an independent state in the Punjab where their holy city, Amritsar, is situated. Here too is located their temple, one of the most beautiful in India.

One could mention many reformers or founders of new sects. One of the more recent trends is the Brahmo Samaj (One God

Society) founded around 1828 by Ram Mohun Roy, a Bengal writer. He was strongly influenced by Western ideas and although he wished to restore Hinduism to its original purity, he borrowed considerably from Christianity. The Brahmo Samaj later divided into the Adi Samaj (the 'original society') and the Sadharen-samaj (the General Society).

One idealistic, nationalistic and extremely forceful figure was Dayanand Sarasivati, who in 1875 founded the Arya-Samaj (Society of Aryans, the Pure Ones). He was the son of a high caste Hindu and received a completely intellectual education. There is also a legend connected with his life. Once, when he was with his father in the temple during the fasting in honour and worship of the image of the god Shiva, he saw that when the rice and flowers had been placed upon the statue and the chanting of the prayers had begun, one after another the tired worshippers closed their eyes and fell asleep. Slowly the singing died away, but Dayanand, who wished to remain awake in order to please the god Shiva, suddenly heard a mouse gnawing in the silence. He saw a mouse running along the statue, carrying away the rice that the faithful had strewn there. He nudged his father then and asked how it was possible that Shiva, if he was truly a god, was not able to chase away a mouse. 'Do not ask questions,' replied his father, 'only an unbeliever asks.' Naturally enough this answer did not satisfy Dayanand. It had suddenly become clear to him that Shiva was merely an object made of stone without any power at all. He left the temple, broke the fast and decided never to adore idols again. He, too, set out into the world, studying and exchanging ideas with teachers of other schools. He made acquaintance with the Christians' Bible, and the Aryan society incorporated in its writings tenets and usages derived from both Hinduism and Christianity.

Here we conclude our, of necessity, brief contact with some of India's philosophical systems and sects. We have by no means mentioned all of them; one can find them dealt with in detail in the monumental work *Der Hinduismus* by the German historian of religions Dr Helmuth von Glasenapp, to which we are indebted for certain points.

Since the history of modern politico-religious Hinduism is inconceivable without the figure of Gandhi, we should like to dwell upon him for a moment.

Gandhi's autobiography, which appeared in Gujarat in 1949 and was translated into English under the title *The Story of My Experiments with Truth*, proved a disappointment to many. The work is in no way profound, and whenever one expects to be given some insight into the basis of Hindu thought or the religious structure of Indian society, the writer lingers on all sorts of incidentals, displaying a certain guileless childishness. We are given copious details concerning his diet, his anxiety about his health, his struggle against physical passions and his experiences in the various trades which he practised. As an autobiography, however, it is fascinating, if only for the figure of the writer who sought the Truth, found it, and scrupulously observed it. As the founder of a free India he can be numbered among the greatest leaders of modern history. His claim to greatness lies chiefly in his non-violent political leadership which was based not on material power but on spiritual authority. He has been compared to Christ and called St Francis of India. It has been mockingly observed that Gandhi became the guilty conscience of all Christians since they wonder what they can show to measure up to the love of truth, the readiness to sacrifice, the self-denial and the love of peace of this wise Indian.

However, although Gandhi was almost universally revered, his political conduct never lacked critics. Gandhi's human weakness lay in a certain opportunism which led him in the Boer War and in the two World Wars to accept compromises which were in direct conflict with his doctrine of non-violence and his absolute pacifism. He explained his support for Great Britain, first in the Boer War and again in the wars of 1914 and 1939, and his call to young Indians to join the British army by arguing that so long as he, as a British citizen, claimed certain rights and protection, it was his duty to share in the defence of the British Empire. He was convinced that India could only gain complete emancipation within and through the British Empire. Gandhi was entirely aware that participation in a war could not be reconciled with the idea of *ahimsa*, the attainment

of a state beyond good or evil. Anyone who is fully involved in
life cannot live a moment without either consciously or unconsciously coming into conflict with this idea. When two nations
are at war it is the duty of every supporter of *ahimsa* to end the
war, but – argued Gandhi – anyone who is not equal to this
duty, who has no power to oppose the war or is not competent
to do so, is justified in taking part in the war. He should, however, sincerely try to free himself, his country and the world
from war.

Gandhi's opponents smiled on reading the following statement made by the Mahatma in his *Experiments with Truth*: 'I
had hoped to improve my status and that of my people through
the British Empire. Whilst in England [in 1914] I was enjoying
the protection of the British fleet, and taking shelter as I did
under its armed might, I was directly participating in its potential violence. Therefore, if I desired to retain my connection
with the Empire and to live under its banner, one of three
courses was open to me: I could declare open resistance to the
war and, in accordance with the law of *satya graha* [passive
resistance], boycott the Empire until it changed its military
policy; or I could seek imprisonment by civil disobedience of
such of its laws as were fit to be disobeyed; or I could participate in the war on the side of the Empire and thereby acquire
the capacity and fitness for resisting the violence of war. I
lacked this capacity and fitness, so I thought there was nothing
for it but to serve in the war.' In the opinion of many the incon-
sequence of this standpoint showed Gandhi to be an extremely
practical politician rather than a leader who abided by his
principles. And yet his *asahayoga* (non-co-operation), his pro-
paganda in favour of the reintroduction of the spinning wheel
in order to combat the import of British cotton and his promotion of Indian cottage industries were spectacular examples of
practical politics as well as romantic gestures which found
their echo in the mass of the people struggling towards self-
determination.

Rabindranath Tagore, who sought to synthesize Eastern and
Western schools of thought, occupies a prominent place in
world literature. His philosophy differed from the usual Indian

view of life in that he did not preach asceticism or a flight from the world, but a losing oneself in God in daily life through joy and love. Tagore (or Thakur, anglicized version of his name) was born in 1861, died in 1941, and received an English as well as an Indian education. He was an exceptionally versatile personality and enjoyed considerable repute as a poet, writer, musician, social reformer and teacher. In 1913 he gained the Nobel Prize for Literature and in 1919 he renounced the knighthood conferred upon him by King George V in protest against the massacre of an unarmed crowd of demonstrators by the British General Dyer in Amritsar. Tagore saw his life's work chiefly in the realization of his ideas concerning the education of youth. He drew up a system which brought young people into the closest possible contact with nature while at the same time providing them with an education which combined the advantages of Eastern and Western knowledge. He attempted to put his ideals into practice in his Santi Niketan school, founded in 1901 at Bolpur near Calcutta. This school has since become a university.

Tagore's words in the *Crown of Hinduism* on the necessity for doing away with the caste system have a prophetic sound: 'In my opinion, the rebirth of the Indian people depends directly and perhaps solely upon the abolition of castes. If Europe required the spiritual shock of the Renaissance and the grim struggle of the Reformation before she could break with the feudal system and the tyrannical conventionalism of the medieval Church, which had done violence to the healthy instincts of humanity, do we then not need to an even greater degree the overwhelming influx of higher social concepts before there can be room for truly political thought? Must we not see before us the greater vision of humanity, so that we may be impelled to shake off the chains which bind our individual lives, before we can dream of national freedom?'

In recent times a considerable falling away from Hinduism has been noted, especially among the former Untouchables, in favour of Christianity and Islam. The last censuses in India have shown that in a period of roughly seventy years the number of Muslims has increased by 85 per cent, while the Hindus have increased by only 35. In Bengal, among other places, the

number of Hindus has sharply declined; in a number of provinces where Muslims were in the minority, their representation
has doubled. A considerable number of Indians have become
converts to Christianity, although even so there are no more
than ten million Christians in a population of three hundred
and eighty million. There have been Christians in India since
the very first centuries of our era, many of whom were convinced that the apostle Thomas in person preached the doctrine
of Christ there. Syrians and Armenians contributed greatly to
the spread of Christianity and with the coming of the Portuguese missionary work went ahead rapidly. At the present time
Roman Catholic, Anglican, Adventist, Methodist and Baptist
and other Protestant missionaries are actively engaged in propagating the faith. In this connection the problem has arisen
whether it is correct to begin with the lower strata of society,
the former pariahs in fact, since this repelled the higher classes,
whereas if one set to work the other way round the example of
the higher castes might have an inspiring influence on the
lower. The Church, however, adopts the viewpoint that from
the very beginning Christianity was preached to all without
distinction of position or class. Since the caste system in India
is doomed to disappear – it is argued – it does not matter to
which caste the converted Hindu formerly belonged.

For the educated Hindu, Christianity, like Hinduism or related religious trends, is one of the many paths which may lead
mankind towards bliss. Most of the ethical dogmas of Christianity are to the Hindu nothing but the Dharma (see pp. 44 f.)
which all religions have in common. The Christian dogmas do
not constitute a stumbling block for the tolerant Hindu, no
matter how little he may think of them from his viewpoint. His
objections to Christianity are not dogmatic but have to do
rather with the Christian's social attitude towards the laws
governing food and caste. A Hindu scholar once wrote: 'If
anyone openly proclaims that Jesus Christ is the son of God or
Muhammad the only Prophet he will have no trouble with
Indian society. But there are hundreds of minor regulations
dealing with eating and drinking which the Christian does not
observe. He is therefore regarded as a low and impure being of
whom it can only be hoped that, in the course of his soul's

transmigrations, he will be reborn as a devout Hindu and will then comply with all the laws.'

Despite this tolerance in purely religious matters, Christianity is regarded by the Hindus as a heresy against which Hinduism must be defended. Christian religious teaching regarding the creation out of nothing, original sin and the eternity of rewards and punishments in the after-life is considered to be at variance with philosophical thought. Hindus have frequently attempted to expose 'the true Hindu content of the Christian dogmas'. In the journal *The Light of Truth* (Siddhanta Dipika) a Hindu writer says: 'When I walk through the churches and cathedrals of England and ponder on the many similarities to and traces of Shivaitism which strike me in every corner of England, I cannot help regarding England as a Shivaistic country.'

On a few occasions the Hindus succeeded in converting Europeans to Hinduism. A celebrated example was that of the British Colonel Stewart who renounced Christianity at the beginning of the last century and embraced Hinduism. Courageously he braved the mocking glances of his compatriots when with flowers and sacrificial vessels he journeyed to the Ganges to perform the solemn ablutions required by the Hindu ritual.

Gandhi was completely receptive to Christianity and there were periods in his life when it seemed to the outsider as though he were inclined to go over to Christianity. He created a sort of 'Indian christology' which, however, did not succeed in freeing Hinduism from its sectarian isolation. He was fiercely opposed to his orthodox co-religionists in his work to abolish the caste system, yet at the same time, by obstinately retaining the existing contrasts with regard to the other Indian religions, he kept Hinduism isolated to a certain extent.

European oriental studies have also contributed in no small measure in changing religious and social ideas in India. The work of the European orientalists has revealed to the Indians themselves the historical origin and development of their religious customs and ideas and has opened the way to a free mode of thought. Western influence has also made itself felt in Indian literature, affecting not only content but form as well. In this connection von Glasenapp states that Hindustani, the language employed nowadays in prose literature, was created artificially through the translations made by Lallujiyi Lal at the request of the English. He created a literary language 'for which the prestige of its inventors compelled recognition'. In the same way the so-called Bengali prose also developed from the language which the missionary Carey and his fellow-workers first used for their Bible translations and for compiling textbooks.

Western man will always find it difficult to enter completely into the mental processes and religious concepts of Brahmins and Hindus, whose religious ideas and rites are set down in hard and fast rules. All customs and usages are considered inviolable since they are regarded as being just as sacred as the religion itself. And even if, in the future, students of Indian culture should unveil further secrets, innumerable mysteries would still remain, inaccessible to Western thought. Only by opening our minds in sensitive understanding shall we be able to grasp something of the deep significance of these countless manifestations in their confusing diversity, in which the exalted and the repulsive, the primitive and the superbly refined have fused to become one. Only then shall we be able to appreciate the wonder of this mysterious world in its extra-ordinary beauty.

SUGGESTIONS FOR FURTHER READING

Macnicol, N., *Hindu Scriptures*, Everyman
Parrinder, E. G., *Upanishads, Gita and Bible*, Faber
Radhakrishnan, S., *The Hindu View of Life*, Allen & Unwin
Sen, K. M., *Hinduism*, Penguin
Wood, E., *Yoga*, Penguin
Zaehner, R. C., *Hinduism*, Oxford

3

BUDDHISM

THE CHRONICLES dealing with the origin of Buddhism sound like an enthralling oriental fairy tale.

Once, long, long ago, in a plain of the Ganges at the foot of the Himalayas, there lived a young prince of the princely family of the Shakyas whose name was Siddhartha Gautama . . .[1] His father was prince of Kapilavastu in Magadhi, a region in the north-eastern part of India. Perhaps he was just an ordinary chieftain, but this would deprive the story of its glamour. Prince Siddhartha lived happily and was contented in his father's palace with his wife Yashodara, who had borne him a son, Rahula, until one evil day his peace of mind was cruelly disturbed. He was then twenty-nine years old.

He was taking his ease in the country when he saw a number of peasants ploughing a field. He was seized by a great compassion when he saw how they worked in the sweat of their brows, and how the oxen strained at the plough. He was even roused to pity by the thought of the countless insects and earthworms killed by the disturbance of the soil. For the first time he began to ponder on the meaning of existence and, sitting beneath a shady tree, he engaged in prolonged meditation.

At the birth of Prince Siddhartha, seven wise men from the Himalayas had said that he bore the 'thirty-two marks of the Great Man' on his body and was destined to become King of the World. When he was twelve he had made a vow seriously to

[1] The teachings of Buddhism are written in both Sanskrit and Pali languages. The two languages account for the variant forms of many names, e.g. Gautama and Gotama, *karma* and *kamma*, Nirvana and Nibbana, in which the first ones are Sanskrit and the second Pali, which is related to the Sanskrit. We shall use the Sanskrit spelling here in this chapter.

study and practise the religion of his fathers and had received instruction from priests. On his return to the court he was caught up again in the carefree and luxurious existence there, and it was thus understandable that the unexpected sight of the toiling peasants made a deep impression on him.

But this was not to be all. Four successive encounters were to bring about a turning point in his life. One glorious morning, as he was out hunting with his servant Channa, he saw an emaciated man lying by the roadside, racked by violent pains. 'What is wrong with this man?' the prince asked his servant. 'The man is sick and suffers pain, my prince,' answered Channa. 'Why is he sick?' asked the prince. 'That is life,' was the answer. 'Anyone may fall sick.' The prince was startled and saddened by the suffering with which he was suddenly confronted.

The next day, when the prince and his servant were again out hunting, they beheld an old man whose back was bowed by age and who hobbled painfully along with the aid of sticks. 'What is wrong with this man?' asked the prince, 'is he sick, too?' 'No,' said Channa, 'he is old and this is the fate of every man as he grows old.' Once again the prince was seized by a feeling of grief and halted the hunt.

The third encounter occurred shortly afterwards when the pair were walking along a country road and met a funeral procession, accompanied by a weeping woman and children. The prince asked what this meant. 'This, my prince, comes to all mortals,' answered the servant. 'It matters not if he is a king or a beggar, death comes to all, whoever they may be.' Sunk in deep thought the prince returned to the palace where his wife had just prepared a banquet. Young maidens danced, and the loud tones of musical instruments resounded. The prince refused to attend the feast, retired to his private apartments and pondered on what he had seen during the last few days. There must be something wrong with life, he thought. How otherwise could it contain so much suffering and sorrow? In the many sacred Books which he had studied he had never come across an explanation of the origin of suffering and adversity. It dawned on him that his own people were divided into rigorously distinct castes. Most of his father's subjects belonged to the lowest caste, and the very poorest were even denied the right to enter the temple. He wondered why the Creator had divided the people into so many castes, which seemed to him an injustice.

One last encounter was to be decisive for him. It took place in the market-square where the prince had mingled with the crowd. Suddenly he saw a monk, dressed in rags, who was begging for food. Although he was old and in a pitiable state, a serene calm and dignified resignation radiated from his features. He was one of the thousands of men in India who had left their homes and their families in order to go up into the mountains, where they lived in silence in order to be able to devote themselves undisturbed to their religion. Every now and then they came down to the cities to beg a little food.

A longing seized the prince to belong to these monks and to spend all his time observing the laws of his faith and pondering on the possibility of showing his people the way to a happier future. He decided thus to leave his palace and his family in order to join the mendicant monks. He had to overcome considerable opposition before he was able to order Channa to saddle his horse. They rode away together, and a little way outside the city the prince ordered Channa to cut off his hair and his beard. He himself removed his jewels. After this they said good-bye and the prince set out upon his long laborious journey in search of the true Wisdom of Life. On the road he met a beggar whom he besought to exchange clothes with him. Thus he embarked upon a new life as a beggar-monk, and the night upon which this occurred was called the Night of the Great Renunciation.

It is exceedingly doubtful whether the reality concerning the life of the prince who was to become Buddha – an Enlightened One – corresponds with this story. The biographies of Buddha are based for the greater part on tradition and were only written many centuries after Buddha's death. Buddha himself left no writings behind him, and one has to rely on the Pali or Sanskrit texts of the Hinayana or the Mahayana, a collective name for the many trends in Buddhism which emerged round A.D. 100. One can also consult the edicts of King Ashoka of the

C

Maurya dynasty, one of the mightiest rulers of India, who reigned from 274 to 237 B.C. Mahayana means 'the greater, better path' (also called the Great Vehicle) in contrast to the Hinayana, 'the small, lesser path' (also called the Little Vehicle) which refers to the earliest school of Buddhism. The essential features of Buddha's biography are, however, accepted as correct.

How did the prince-beggar monk fare further? For seven years he wandered from place to place in search of the Wisdom which would enable him to solve the enigma of life. He had a number of important encounters, including one with King Bimbisara of Magadha, who wished to make him his personal adviser. This was an honourable offer, which he naturally rejected. 'If I had sought wealth and honour,' he said, 'I could have been king in the kingdom of my father.' He consulted Brahman philosophers like Alara and Uddaka. 'Teach me to know the Wisdom of the World,' he asked. 'Study the Vedas (the oldest sacred books of the Brahmins and Hindus, written in Sanskrit, see pp. 40 ff.) for they contain all Wisdom,' they both replied.

On one occasion five monks crossed his path; they, too, were in search of Wisdom. In order to find it – they judged – we must purify our souls, and to attain this purity we must torture our bodies and starve ourselves. Together they all went into a dense wood where they chastised themselves and abstained from food until their bodies were as thin as skeletons and they could scarcely walk. Siddhartha, too, was practically exhausted and lost consciousness. His companions thought that he was dead, but when he revived he explained that he had come to realize that this was not the right way to obtain worldly wisdom. He would begin to eat again and regain his strength in order to be able to think clearly. The monks censured him for this decision, which they regarded as weakness, and went away, leaving him alone.

For months he wandered through the woods and beside the fields, living on fruit and rice given to him by people who took pity on him. Seated under a fig tree – the sacred fig tree of Gaya – lost in meditation, he gradually came to realize that he was wrongly seeking something which lay outside his own self. He realized that he could not acquire it by studying the Vedas, by suffering hunger or by mortifying himself. He must seek it in himself, and only in himself would he find it. Just as Jesus in the desert withstood the three temptations of the devil, the mendicant monk succeeded in repelling the assaults of Mara, the evil spirit who embodied death and the world of the senses. Then, all at once, the great Wisdom he had sought was revealed to him. This spiritual awakening is called *Bodhi*, from which is derived the word Buddha, meaning enlightened or awakened. This wisdom was revealed to him in three forms: knowledge concerning his former existences; knowledge of the former existences of all other beings, the so-called 'heavenly gaze'; and the formula of the twelve *nidanas* which became the basis of the Buddhist doctrine. These *nidanas* are depicted in the Wheel of Existence, also called the Wheel of the Norm. This is a representation in pictures of the Buddhist philosophy.

But still Buddha's mind was not entirely at rest. For seven more days he remained alone under the fig tree, meditating on the 'first law of life' and upon the wisdom which he had acquired through it. When he judged that his thoughts were sufficiently clear in his mind, he decided to go out into the world to propagate his doctrine. He went first of all to the city of Benares. There he saw the five monks who had deserted him before and who like him had been searching for Truth but had not yet found it. They asked him now whither his thinking had led him. To this Buddha replied: 'Listen, it has become clear to me that the first law of life is: good must come from good and evil from evil. Everything in life is subject to this law.' The monks accepted this wisdom with some hesitation; they were of the opinion that this was 'nothing new'. Thereupon Buddha continued: 'Water always flows downhill, ice is always cold, fire is always hot. Praying to all the gods in India will not make water flow uphill, ice become hot or fire cold. This is because there are laws of life which make things as they are, so that all that is done cannot be made to become undone. Prayers and sacrifices to the gods must therefore be useless. If all our idols have no power to change anything in the world, then they ought not to be adored. If a man does good, the results of his action will be good, if he does evil then the results will be evil. The adoration of idols is wrong and foolish.'

The monks were obliged to acknowledge that Buddha's argument was valid, whereupon Buddha, taking advantage of the hour at which they were receptive to his words, continued: 'If you agree with this, then the Vedas, which exhort people to adore idols, are not sacred books. Sacred books ought not to teach that which is wrong and untrue. Our priests declare that every word in the Vedas is sacred, but I proclaim that the Vedas are not sacred books. They teach us that Brahma has divided the people into castes. This is not correct, by virtue of the first law of life. People are only divided into good and bad; those who are good are good, and those who are bad are bad. It makes no difference what family they were born to.' And, to the amazement of the monks who were listening with rapt attention, Buddha spoke the decisive words: 'I do not believe that Brahma created anything, not even the world. *The world was always there*. The world will exist for ever and never come to an end. And something which has no end has no beginning.'

After a time Buddha summed up his argument in the Four Noble Truths. The first is the universal fact of suffering: to exist is to suffer; suffering is caused by selfish desire; selfish desire can be eliminated; this can be done by following the 'Noble Eightfold Path': right views (the insight that truth is man's guide); right attitude of mind or motive (by never harming any living being); right speech (never speak an untruth and never use rough and coarse language); right conduct (never steal or kill or do anything over which one might later have remorse or of which one might be ashamed); right means of livelihood (never to perform a bad act such as forgery, the receiving of stolen goods, or the practice of usury); right effort (strive towards what is good and always refrain from what is evil); right mind-control (concentration) (never to lose one's calm and never to allow oneself to be overcome by joy or sorrow); and right meditation or serenity (this is found when all the other rules are followed and a person has attained the stage of perfect peace).

Deeply impressed by this speech, which up to this day is known as the Sermon at Benares, the monks bowed down before Siddhartha Gautama and declared that they wished to become his disciples since he had set in motion the Wheel of

Existence (Rebirth) which teaches mankind that the world is ruled by Law (Righteousness) and had so become the En-lightened One, the Buddha.

When the five monks had taken a vow to observe the com-mandments of integrity, Buddha formed them into a Brother-hood and thus was Buddhism born. For forty years they travelled up and down the country, propagating their doctrine and gathering an increasing number of followers. Buddha died in his eightieth year; the year of his death is usually taken as 477 B.C. (some think 483 B.C.). His body was cremated according to custom; the remains, such as the ashes, the teeth and what was left of the bones, were divided into eight (or ten) parts, and deposited in reliquary chambers (*stupas*) in eight (or ten) different parts of the country. These are massive stone monu-ments which are accounted among the earliest Buddhist struc-tures.

It is said that Buddhism was originally not a religion in the literal sense since there is no question of a divinity. It was based upon fundamental dogmas and denied the existence of a supreme God as creator of the universe. None the less it did nothing to combat belief in countless gods, spirits and demons, although Buddha himself always refused to acknowledge them. His teaching, which to a certain extent turns away from life, considering it disastrous in all its manifestations, none the less points the way to liberation and redemption from the endless cycle of existences. He who attains this liberation has the cer-tainty that he will not be born again after his death, since he has already been redeemed during his lifetime. 'He has cast aside all sensual desires,' writes Professor Vogel, 'he has freed him-self from the ties of the world, has purified himself of all taints and attained a state of complete detachment in which he is aware of the transience of all phenomena. He who has attained this state of bliss is an *arhat*, a saint.'

Buddhism developed directly from Brahmanism; one might even say that it is a buddhification of Brahmanism. For the Buddhist the problem is: how can I struggle free of the *sam-*

sara (which means literally 'faring on in the stream of worldly [transcendental] life'); how can I free myself from the cycle of rebirths, from the suffering into which man is plunged as a result of his desire for the earthly, for that which does not exist because it is only seeming? The origin of this desire is the longing to cling to life, the will to live which will not be suppressed. The nature of our existence is determined by our earlier forms of existence, and every desire assumes a different shape in a new form of existence, until the stage is reached when we become detached from all that binds us to life. This is the law of *karma* which, together with the concept of reincarnation, is especially prominent in Theosophy. The word *karma* means action, deeds, in the sense of action-reaction, cause and effect. Applied to man, the law of *karma* teaches that every person is the creator of his own fate, it is the result of his actions and still more the result of the motives which impelled him to these particular actions. The cycle of rebirths implies that everyone has to pass through several forms of existence before attaining Nirvana, extinction of individuality and absorption into the supreme spirit. Attainment of Nirvana is preceded by perfect inner peace, the destruction of all desire, and this can be achieved even during one's lifetime.

Buddha is said to have lived through five hundred and thirty lives before reaching the status of 'Enlightened One'. He was twenty-four times a prince, eighty-five times a king, twenty-two times a scholar, forty-two times a god, twice a thief, once a slave and many times a lion, a horse, an eagle and a snake. All these stories are contained in the Jataka Tales, translated into English by the British orientalist T. W. Rhys Davies from Pali language, in which part of the Buddhist canonical writings and many literary works are composed. The stories, which all refer to Buddha's life before he became an Enlightened One (after this he was no longer reborn but entered into Nirvana), are fairly naïve. Thus it happened that Buddha, when he was a bird, lived in a wood surrounded by a flock of birds in a shady tree with branches which stuck out in all directions. One day a lot of dust fell on the branches which rubbed against each other, sending up a quantity of smoke. The Buddha-bird thought: if the branches continue to rub against each other, sparks will fly, a fire will start which will spread to the dried leaves and the tree will soon be consumed by the fire. We cannot prevent this, so we must leave this place and seek another. He spoke to the other birds (in verse) and told them of their danger. A few of the birds were sensible, listened to Buddha and went away. Others, however, mocked his advice and said that he had already seen 'crocodiles in a drop of water' on more than one occasion. So they remained. Not long afterwards the tree burst into flames, and the birds were blinded by the fire, could no longer fly away and so perished lamentably.

Even during Buddha's lifetime disputes frequently flared up among his followers. As a rule Buddha refused to become involved, warning them of the dangers of dividedness in the hope that they themselves would find the way to settle their differences. This hope often proved vain, so that Buddha had to resort to telling a sort of 'parable' which was supposed to make the monks think again. One of these stories has come down to us, the tale of Prince Dirghayu. It goes like this: In former times there lived in Benares a mighty king called Brahmadatta of Kashi. He went to war against Durgheti, King of Kosala, because he thought that the kingdom of Kosala was small and would offer no resistance to his armies. And indeed, when Durgheti saw that resistance was impossible, he fled, leaving his kingdom in the hands of Brahmadatta. After much wandering he arrived secretly with his wife in Benares, and settled in the home of a potter, a little way outside the city. There the queen bore a son who was given the name Dirghayu.

Dirghayu flourished, and when he grew to be a young man his father feared that King Brahmadatta, who was of a vengeful nature, would murder him, his wife and his son if he came to hear that they were living in Benares. Accordingly he sent Dirghayu, who had been excellently brought up, out into the wide world. And indeed it came about that King Durgheti was betrayed by his former barber, who recognized him. The king and queen were seized and condemned to death. On the way to the place of execution the king saw his son among the crowd; he had come intending to visit his parents. The king, who did not wish to reveal his son's presence yet wanted to impart to

him one last piece of advice, cried out loudly, without looking
in his son's direction: 'Dirghayu my son, do not tarry too long
with hatred and do not act too hastily, for hatred is not conquered by hatred but only by renouncing hatred.' The king and
queen were horribly done to death, but Dirghayu their son
bought a quantity of strong wine, got the guards drunk and,
when night had fallen, cremated his parents' remains with every
mark of honour and according to the religious rites.

King Brahmadatta learned what had happened and feared
that Dirghayu would avenge the death of his parents by mur-
dering him. This was indeed Dirghayu's intention when he presented himself at the palace some time later. A lad was required
in the elephant stables and he was taken on by the head groom.
One day King Brahmadatta heard singing in the stables and
was struck by the clarity and purity of the voice. He was told
that the singer was a young man who had been recently employed. The king sent for Dirghayu, commanded him to sing,
then gave him a position in his palace. It was not long before
the king, who valued the young man's wisdom, conscientious-
ness and discretion, appointed him to a position of trust.

But then it happened that the king was out hunting and
became separated from the rest of his companions. Only Dirghayu remained by his side. At noon they lay down and the king
was soon fast asleep. Then Dirghayu thought: King Brahmadatta has done us much harm, he stole our kingdom and had
my parents murdered. Now he is in my power. And he was
already drawing his sword to kill the king when he remembered
the words of his father: 'Do not tarry too long with hatred and
do not act too hastily, for hatred is not conquered by hatred but
only by renouncing hatred.' On recalling these words he
lowered his sword and returned it to its scabbard. The king's
sleep was disturbed, and when he awoke Dirghayu asked him
whether perhaps he had had a fearful dream. The king replied
that his sleep was always disturbed because he often dreamed
that Prince Dirghayu, whom he had never seen, would avenge
his parents. He had just had this dream again. At this Dirghayu
revealed who he was and said that the king was now in his
power. The king begged him to spare his life. 'How can I do
that?' answered Dirghayu, 'you know now who I am and so

you will surely have me put to death.' Whereupon the king said: 'Dirghayu, grant me my life and I will spare yours,' and they promised that each would spare the other's life. The king, however, could not refrain from asking Dirghayu what his father had meant by the words which he had spoken before his death. Then the young man explained his father's words: 'By "do not tarry too long" my father meant "do not cherish your feelings of hatred too long", by "do not act too hastily" he meant "do not be too hasty in enmity with your friends" for hatred cannot be conquered by hatred but only by renouncing hatred. You, O king, had my father and my mother killed. If I should take your life then your followers would take mine and my followers would feel obliged to kill yours. Hatred would thus not be conquered by hatred. But now you have granted me my life as I have granted you yours so that hatred is conquered by not-hating.' Astonished by the wisdom of these words King Brahmadatta of Kashi returned the kingdom of Kosala to Prince Dirghayu and in addition gave him his daughter in marriage.

In this and similar traditional stories emerges the central idea of Buddhism which may sound, to our modern ears, somewhat milk-and-watery: tolerance, love of peace, a sense of community, a lack of envy, dispute and above all the promotion of 'goodwill'. These virtues can only be acquired by self-denial, spiritual and moral discipline and subjection to the supreme authority. According to the descriptions, Buddha seems to have possessed two qualities which are seldom encountered together in one person: on the one hand he possessed a great love for humanity, endless patience, unfailing affability and a strong spiritual force; on the other he was a thinker, a brilliant philosopher who penetrated to the heart of all that was positive and negative in the thinking of his day, accepting that which seemed to him right and healthy and rejecting what in his eyes conflicted with the true and the good. According to its supporters Buddhism is the only one of the great world religions to be deliberately based upon a systematic, rational analysis of the problem of life and of the way in which this problem may be resolved. The critics, on the other hand, object that, although

Buddhism is a doctrine of love which preaches compassion and benevolence towards all living creatures, this inner fervour is in reality nothing but sentimentality and melancholy. Buddhism, they say, lacks a moral task, and it is this fact that renders it so negative and so passive. By taking only an intellectual interest in the fate of one's fellow men, one remains basically detached from it. Buddhism is, in their view, the religion of inertia, whereby one perceives moral and material shortcomings with the mind but does nothing about them.

Buddhism spread throughout the world fairly rapidly. Two centuries after Buddha's death the new religion had not only penetrated to extensive regions in India but had also gained a foothold in the neighbouring countries. For a thousand years Buddhism was a powerful force in the formation of the religious, moral, artistic and social life of India. At the end of this thousand years the decay set in, and a good five hundred years later it had practically disappeared, at least from its country of origin. It remained, however, the predominant religion in Ceylon, Burma, Thailand and in some parts of south-east Asia where it has maintained its position up to the present day. In Sumatra, Java, Borneo and Celebes, however, it was confronted with the rising tide of Islam and retreated. It became one of the living religions in China and Korea, gained Tibet entirely and succeeded in obtaining a place in the religious life of Japan.

Buddhism, too, has its schools, the most important of which are the Hinayana and the Mahayana. The Hinayana is considered as the original Buddhism which began its missionary activity around 250 B.C. This task was undertaken by the Bhikkhus or mendicant monks who had formed an order. Robed in habits and carrying their begging bowls, they set out to propagate their faith. The monasteries were the centre of an intense spiritual life. Conditions were rigorous, and existence was hard. No object might be regarded as personal property, everything belonged to the community. Only sandals were permitted as footwear. The head was shaved, even among the nuns, for besides the order of monks there also existed an order of nuns, to which Buddha had originally objected. However, strong pressure was put upon him to admit women, too, in the first place by the women in his entourage, but especially by Ananda, his cousin and most exemplary disciple. Ananda was renowned for his excellent memory which enabled him to write down the many conversations he had with his master. When Ananda, in all humility, asked Buddha did he not think that women too, by leading a chaste and pious life, could share in the *arhat* (sainthood), Buddha agreed and gave permission for nunneries to be founded.

Payapati, Buddha's aunt, his mother's sister, was the first to be admitted to the 'houseless life'. Once the Order of Sisters was founded, however, it grew rapidly. Countless girls and young women who heard of the Revelation of Buddha, of the Truth of the Law and of the Eightfold Path towards overcoming the consequences of the fact that life, for the greater part, consists of painful experiences, were gripped by the idea. They left their husbands or their parental homes in order to lead a pure and virtuous life. They were impelled, however, not so much by a feeling of sin as by an intuitive insight into the transience of all human institutions. Entrance to the nunnery which involved a farewell to the world was for them a liberation, a deliverance from the restraining influences upon their spiritual development. The childless widows, often an object of contempt in those days, sinful women, rich men's wives who were frittering away their lives in useless idleness, young girls who were subjected to the humiliation of being married off to the highest bidder, all 'chose freedom' with its stern obligations and physical deprivations.

Several biographies of Buddhist nuns have been written; they usually end with a sort of song or psalm written by the actual nun concerned. In Psalm XVIII, by Sister Sangha, for example, one can read: 'I gave up my home, for I abandoned the world; I gave up my child and my favourite flocks; desire has gone and hate has disappeared; ignorance is now far from me; thirst and the cause of thirst have been overcome; now I am cool and free, tasting perfect inner peace.'

A number of convents were built and they were regarded as being on an equal footing with the monasteries. Some enjoyed considerable esteem, and Buddha frequently referred to them as models of virtue and spiritual worthiness. At the present time there are still many Buddhist nunneries in Burma. They disappeared centuries ago in Ceylon, but around 1920 a number of them were revived, thanks to the initiative of a devout woman, Sister Soedhammachari, descended from a noble Sinhalese family which had become Christian under Portuguese, Dutch and British domination. Her mother, however, had remained a Buddhist and although Soedhammachari was educated in the Christian faith she felt herself so strongly attracted to Buddhism that she made a profound study of the doctrine and the holy scriptures. When her only son was reared (she had become a widow at an early age) she decided to devote herself entirely to the Buddhist thinking. She studied for eight years in various monasteries in Burma, learned Sanskrit and Pali and was finally received into the Order. She then returned to Ceylon where, with the financial support of Lady Blake, the wife of the British Governor, she bought a simple house in Kandy and established a convent there. In 1924 she was already working with twenty sisters, chiefly teaching poor children and caring for the sick. The remaining hours of the day were filled with meditation, alternating with visits to the Temple.

The texts and precepts of Buddhism were definitely established at three Councils. The first was held shortly after Buddha's death at Rajagriha, the ancient capital of Maghada, and served to revise and draw up a definitive text of the Vinaya Pitaka, dealing with monastic discipline. Five hundred monks, the prescribed number, took part in this Council. A number of scribes, including Ananda, were consulted. A hundred years later the Council of Vesali met, when the movement split into two groups, the *Mahasanghikas* ('Members of the Great Community') and the *Sthaviras* ('Supporters of the Teaching of the Elders'). In the course of time the first group produced five schools, the second eleven. All these schismatics were of considerable importance in the further development of Buddhism.

The third Council, held at Pataliputra, met under the auspices of King Ashoka, about 250 B.C. Ashoka's name is closely associated with the first flourishing of Buddhism which found in him a convinced and devoted supporter. Ashoka began his career as a ruler of great coarseness and cruelty;

Scheltema & Holkema's
BOEKHANDEL

AMSTERDAM - ROKIN 74 - 76   FILIAAL: GRIMBURGWAL 4
POSTGIRO 812 - GEM. GIRO S 5682

DATUM .... 17 5 ....19 ..

Allesrino
die
World
Religion   4 75

PARAGON AMSTERDAM   VERK.
357638   ƒ

after his conversion his character became one of gentle tolerance, coupled with a strong aversion to force and war-like
exploits. Only religious conquests had true value in his eyes
and he contrasted victories gained with the sword with the
conquest made by the Dharma, the law which Buddha had
preached. His mildness was expressed in his fourteen edicts
which he had carved in stone. Several of these have been discovered in modern times. They contain recommendations concerning respect for life, refraining from violence and the use of
coarse language. These edicts are signed with the name Pujadasi
which Ashoka had probably assumed on succeeding to the
throne. Ashoka did a great deal for the development of his
country; it is noted in particular that he had trees planted and
imported medicinal herbs. He abhorred hunting and amusement and also disapproved of slaughtering animals for ceremonial feasts. He urged generosity towards non-Buddhists and
taught that children should be obedient and respect their
parents. He deeply regretted having conquered the country of
Kalinga by force in the ninth year of his reign, causing the
death or deportation of many thousands of people. His remorse
was great because he had thereby sinned against the principles
of human dignity.

It is not certain that King Ashoka was indeed 'converted' to
Buddhism on the island of Ceylon in the spectacular manner
mentioned in a number of chronicles. He did, however, act as
the leader of the Buddhist community and summoned the
Council of Pataliputra in order to rid the various Buddhist
communities of 'heretics'. In one of his edicts he says: 'You
all know how great is my respect for and devotion to Buddha,'
and he goes on: 'All that the Lord Buddha has said was well
said.' Ashoka undertook numerous pilgrimages to holy places.
He visited Sarnath, near Benares, where Buddha is tradition-
ally thought to have started his teaching. He went to the Lumbini Gardens near Kapilavastu where Buddha was born, and
there he knelt down and pronounced the words: 'Happy are
they and blessed who have seen the great Wise One and who
have heard his sweet words.'

The discovery of a number of rock-edicts and messages
carved on pillars, the text of which was composed in the

regional dialect, has contributed in no small measure to the knowledge of Indian philology. In 1893, for example, the lower part of a pillar was discovered at Lumbini, containing Ashoka's inscription after his visit there. In 1905 scholars unearthed at Sarnath the shaft of a pillar crowned with four lions, which dates from the period of Ashoka's presence at this place.

We spoke of the two great trends in Buddhism, the Hinayana, referring to the original Buddhism, and the Mahayana, the collective name for the various schools. In his work *The Teachings of the Compassionate Buddha*, Professor E. A. Burtt also calls the Hinayana the Theravada Buddhism. He defines the word Theravada as 'the way of the elders'. At the present day Theravada Buddhism predominates in Ceylon, Burma and Thailand. The doctrine is recorded in the *Tripitaka*, which consists of three parts: first, the disciplinary rules; second, the explanation of Buddha's teaching; and third, various scholastic interpretations. Many contrasts may be discerned between Hinayana and Mahayana, just as numerous contrasts exist between the various schools which have imparted to Buddhism its practically boundless spiritual wealth. However, if we were to deal with all these schools we would far exceed the scope of this chapter.

The Mahayana, which is viewed as a new doctrine of redemption, gave an entirely new interpretation of Buddha's teaching. The cardinal points were: (1) that Siddhartha Gautama, the historical Buddha, was one of the many manifestations of the divine in the world, and (2) the appearance of the so-called Bodhisattvas, whose powers were almost equal to Buddha, who had the fate of mankind at heart and were invoked in times of need. Professor J. P. Vogel writes that the word was originally the honorary title of the great being who was destined to become Buddha. 'The Bodhi, the spiritual awakening, first made him Buddha, the Enlightened One; before the Bodhi he was called Bodhisattva, i.e. he who bears within him the essence of the Bodhi.' . . . And also: 'He was given the name Bodhisattva not only in his last existence up to the moment of the Bodhi, but also in the numerous existences which preceded this. In the chief of these former births he has distinguished himself by deeds of great self-sacrifice which have rendered him worthy finally to attain the Buddhahood.'

For people had long held the opinion that Siddhartha Gautama had had a series of predecessors who had proclaimed the same doctrine. Whenever decline threatened and the right teaching had lapsed, a new redeemer appeared who restored the doctrine to its original purity. There had been six predecessors altogether and the Buddha-to-come had already been named in case Siddhartha Gautama's doctrine should decline. The Buddha-to-come is Maitreya, to whom Buddhists turn as the future bringer of salvation according to the theory of the ever recurrent cycles of the universe. There will, however, also be 'Buddhas for themselves alone' who, having attained enlightenment, keep it for themselves. One who is 'perfectly enlightened' communicates his teaching to the people.

Among the supporters of the Mahayana there sprang up again a number of circles, including those which taught the 'perfection of perfect wisdom' and postulated the relativity of all things. One of the greatest of these teachers was Nagarjuna, in the second century A.D., who developed the thesis that the perceptible world does not really exist but is merely a figment of the imagination, a delusion. An absolute reality does exist, but it cannot be expressed in words and is subject only to a mystical approach. Nagarjuna founded the so-called school of the Middle Path which denied both the existence and the non-existence of things.

New concepts, ideas, views and dialectic theories succeeded each other and found convinced adepts. Various opinions were held concerning Buddha's life as a historical personality. For example, three Buddha bodies were distinguished: the cosmic body which was held to be equal to absolute being; the body of perfect bliss, which was thought to be the previous body in a more personal appearance (sometimes compared with the Western concept of God); and the transformation body, the form which Buddha assumed to appear among people on earth.

Not all the texts of the Mahayana Buddhism possess the same authority for all Buddhists. The old teaching confined itself strictly to what was of value for the Redemption, and postu-

lated that the solution of the problems with which man is constantly being confronted was beyond its powers. The Mahayan-
ists did not always respect this limit; they stressed the nothingness (void) of all existence, the better to be able to point the
way to perfect enlightenment. Buddha pointed the way but did
not redeem. The old teaching left man to confront this task
alone; no god can nullify the results of the *karma*; suffering
man must realize that suffering is an inherent part of existence.
Did not Buddha say in his sermon at Benares that birth is
suffering, old age is suffering, sickness and death are suffering?
The 'thirst for a permanent individual existence' may be
quenched by mental concentration which may be attained
through meditation.

Some of Buddha's wise and beautiful sayings were written
down and have been preserved up to the present day. 'Suffering
never originates spontaneously,' said Buddha, 'man is the
cause of his own suffering.' 'Never become attached to anything
that is born of Time.' Again: 'Life knows neither forgiveness
nor vengeance, there is always harmony, it knows no time; the
great evil is the darkness of ignorance which mistakes the
seeming for reality, thus arousing desires, a source of grief for
every being.'

The philosophy of Buddhism is regarded as the most profound and elevated of all philosophies. It has, moreover, influenced Western thought in our day much as did the Greek
philosophical schools centuries earlier. Like Buddhism itself,
the Buddhist philosophy accepts the limitations of our powers
of comprehension. It has no elaborate system of metaphysics.
It takes the view that the knowledge of the origin and essence
of things remains unattainable to us and that it is senseless to
try to acquire or to explore it. Preoccupation with these questions is not only useless but even harmful and reprehensible,
since it is a vain waste of time. Knowledge is only important
to us in so far as it broadens our insight concerning the origin
and relief of suffering.

The Buddhist philosophers have constantly reiterated that
there can be no question of a personal immortality. For there
is no such thing as an independent, indivisible soul, no un-
changing Self, there is merely a series of changing images, of

successive states of consciousness. Of these is our Self composed. Consequently our personality never remains consistent but is constantly changing. It cannot be supposed that we should form a fixed and independent unit in the midst of all that is transient. It is this delusion which lies at the root of man's desirous striving and thus of all his wretchedness. It follows thus that where no independent soul exists there is no room either for an independent continued existence of that soul; something that is constantly changing cannot possibly continue to exist eternally in a definite form. The hope for personal immortality can only be equated with egoism, an attachment to one's own individual existence. One can, however, speak of a moral immortality which is embodied in the *karma* teaching.

Buddhist philosophy concentrates to a certain extent on *suffering* which is viewed as the basic theme of earthly life. The Buddhist teaching can only be of value to or accepted by those who regard life as suffering. To those who do not view life in this manner, it must appear an absurdity. Many years ago Dr C. J. Wijnaendts Francken pointed out the great points of difference between Buddhism and Christianity in this respect. Christianity regards suffering as punishment for sin, not only for one's own sins but for those of one's forbears. Suffering is at the same time a means of improvement and of attaining moral perfection, 'a necessary stage in the earthly period if later heavenly bliss is to be obtained'. In Buddhism suffering proceeds from life itself, it is 'a necessary component of every striving'; it is a consequence of the iron law of causality, not of guilt in the Christian style, i.e. of a sin in the sense of revolt against God. 'Instead of the theological-metaphysical concept *sin* we have the realistic-psychological concept *suffering*.'

It is necessary to eliminate desire, to acquire complete detachment if we are not to be dominated by suffering. Love, too, is evil if it is applied to the individual. 'He who loves a hundred-fold also suffers a hundred-fold; only he who neither loves nor hates is freed from all chains. Where nothing is cherished there is no cause for sadness. Happy and unconcerned are they, therefore, who hold nothing in the world dear.'

Dr Wijnaendts Francken, who did not regard Buddhism as a religion in the true sense (it nowhere preaches the existence of a God), or as a philosophical system since it abstains from any metaphysics, saw it as a moral philosophy, an attitude to life, an interweaving of religious elements and intellectual ideas. He summed up its meaning as follows: Buddhists recognize only a series of phases which are eternal and transitory. The soul, too, is nothing but a changeable structure of states of consciousness. Our ignorance gives rise to false notions regarding our personality and leads to an incessant striving and desiring. This striving and desire leads to endless suffering. This suffering can only be relieved by the quenching of the life of the will; it finds complete annihilation in the Nirvana, the doctrine of enlightenment through absorption into Nothingness.

Dr Wijnaendts Francken dealt analytically but by no means critically with the complete absence of a belief in God or of a divine revelation. The concept of God is not even disputed and the existence of God not even denied. There is no question of a creation in the Old Testament sense, of a loving Father, of prayer or the efficacy of prayer. In the eyes of the Buddhists it would be foolishness to assume that any of these could change the course of the world. A refraining from any active striving, the avoidance of any manifestation of the life impulse here on earth as the Westerner knows it, form the chief characteristics of Buddhist morality. This conduces, according to Dr Wijnaendts Francken, to an indifference to social problems and a lack of historical consciousness but at the same time to a state of tranquillity and a contemplative attitude to life which contrast sharply with the feverish and hunted tempo of life in the West which is constantly fabricating new needs and new desires and thus rendering man more sensitive to suffering.

Alongside the philosophy of Buddhism, which covers wide terrain and has as its principal concept the 'theory of the Void' (the negation of Being), there is also an extensive literature. The arts of poetry, architecture, sculpture and painting are also of considerable importance and derive their interest in a large measure from their wealth of symbolic images. Representations of Buddha, scenes from the life of Buddha, the remains of pieces of sculpture and tenets expressed in concrete works of art, form part of the precious collections of museums throughout the world.

The field of ancient East Asiatic artistic expression is immense, and it would be foolhardy to attempt to convey even a general impression within the scope of this short study. Buddha's life has been described and depicted in countless forms. One of the most fascinating examples of Buddhist art is the so-called Lalita-Vistara on the main wall of the first gallery of the Borobadur, the Buddhist sanctuary on the island of Java, which is not a temple but a *stupa* (chamber). The meaning of the name Borobadur is uncertain: it could mean either 'the many Buddhas' or 'the Buddha sanctuary'. The monument is covered with reliefs, inscriptions, symbols, magical representations and depictions of Buddha.

We are all familiar with the similar, almost traditional Buddha figures, but on closer inspection it appears that a great diversity of representation exists and that, for example, the Buddha figures from Burma differ considerably in physical features, clothing and headdress from the sober monk-like figures of Java and Ceylon. None the less a Buddha figure is immediately recognizable by certain physical characteristics, including the protuberance of the skull and the small growth of hair between the eyebrows. The hair is arranged in curling tresses. Other characteristics are the long ear lobes, deformed by the wearing of heavy golden ear ornaments when Buddha was still living a princely life as a *Bodhisattva*. There is in addition the wheel symbol on the palms of the hands and the soles of the feet with finally sloping shoulders and fat belly, etc. This last, however, is most incorrect. There is indeed a 'fat-bellied Buddha' but he is not in fact the Buddha but Po-tai, the fat-bellied god of fortune or fertility. He seems to have been one of Buddha's first eighteen disciples, but he is by no means a Buddha himself. Buddha is so depicted in the (horrible) modern porcelain of Buddha statuettes, and one marvels that it is precisely this unaesthetic figure which has become so popular. The true Buddha is always rendered in aesthetic style, with slim lines, sumptuous head-gear and tranquil, charming features. In the earliest Buddha statues the eyes are usually open; it is only about the fifth century A.D. that one finds them half closed in meditation.

There are many pious legends in circulation concerning the origin of the first statue of Buddha. It seems certain, however, that Buddha was never depicted during the first centuries following his preaching. It was only in A.D. 150 that an iconography of the Exalted One was attempted.

In Buddhist art one finds on the one hand compositions which radiate a noble resignation and tranquillity, while on the other one comes across works which testify to an unbridled imagination, seeking outlet in the shaping of furious figures impelled by the force of their wild passions. Besides the *stupas* with their gates and the granite pillars, a number of monasteries have been preserved. They were carved out of the rock and date from the first century B.C. They contain wall paintings and sculptures, and since they were inhabited for a number of centuries during which the inmates were constantly working to perfect their beauty, one has the opportunity to view the artistic products of different centuries and of various kinds side by side.

There exists a close link between all the art forms of the Asiatic civilizations, but the main accent falls on music. The foundations, laid thousands of years ago, display a number of aspects of which the mythical and legendary and the religious and metaphysical are considered the most important. Of the music of Arabia, Persia and India, only the last has remained entirely free of Western influences. The composers were for the most part also poets and 'holy men'; Rabindranath Tagore wrote hundreds of songs. His *Jana-Gana-Mana* has become the national anthem of modern independent India which possesses a great variety of popular and ceremonial music. This is usually played during feasts or at the bringing in of the harvest. In 1953 the Asian Music Circle was founded in London. Its aim is to introduce Asiatic music to the West.

The growth of trade relations between India and the Far East led to a considerable expansion of Buddhist art. It reached China through East Turkistan and by the sea routes penetrated deep into modern Indonesia. In this way modern man has come into the possession of the loveliest works of art from this distant past, statues of the Buddha, paintings, symbolical representations from different periods, synoptic scenes, the most delicate and sensitive yet at the same time the most robust and passionate works of art of days long gone.

The causes which led to the decline of Buddhism during the four centuries from 800 to 1200 were numerous. Brahmanism held more widespread appeal than the 'unreal' Buddhas, which were too abstract for the imagination of many to grasp. An additional factor was a certain decay in monastic life, where worldly customs crept in. Buddhism may indeed have lacked what we would nowadays call the popular approach and demanded too much self-discipline of the individual who proved incapable of sublimating his inner self without strict guidance. Islam, with its tremendous impetus, gained ground; the Muslim doctrine of obligations, the social and moral laws of Islam fascinated the faithful and set their feet on a firm and clearly sign-posted way.

Yet Buddhism was by no means dead. It lived on not only in India but also in Ceylon, Burma, Siam (Thailand), Indochina and finally in Tibet, where it became the state religion under the name of Lamaism (*lama* is the Tibetan term for monk). The word Lamaism has also become fairly familiar to the present-day reader through the personality of the Dalai Lama, the spiritual head of the Tibetans, who is now in exile in India.

The basis of the whole of Buddha's teaching was compassion for humanity which was hardened in sin and suffered accordingly. He gave moving expression to this compassion in the words which he spoke 'to his children' and which are included by way of Epilogue in Burtt's book *The Teachings of the Compassionate Buddha* which we have already mentioned, and on which the following version is based:

My children, since the Enlightened One (Buddha) saw humanity drowning in the Great Sea of Birth, Death and Sorrow and since he longed to save it, he was filled with compassion;

When he saw the people of the world straying onto wrong paths with nobody to guide them, he was filled with compassion;

When he saw them writhing in the slime of the five sensual lusts in dissolute abandon, he was filled with compassion;

When he saw how they were chained to their wealth, their wives and their children, not knowing how to detach themselves from them, he was filled with compassion;

When he saw how they did evil with the hand, the heart and the tongue and how they frequently plucked the bitter fruits of their sin, yet none the less continued to yield to their desires, he was filled with compassion;

When he saw how they quenched their thirst for the five lusts, even with contaminated water, he was filled with compassion;

When he saw how, although they longed for happiness, they did not make happiness a *karma* (see p. 70) for themselves and how, although they abhorred pain, they yet made of pain a *karma* for themselves and how, although they desired the joys of heaven, they refused to obey his commands on earth, he was filled with compassion;

When he saw how they feared birth, old age and death and yet continued those activities that lead to birth, old age and death, he was filled with compassion;

When he saw how they were consumed by the fires of pain and sorrow, not knowing where to seek the still waters of *samadhi* (complete concentration), he was filled with compassion;

When he saw how they lived in evil times, subject to tyrannical kings and suffering many adversities, yet still carelessly pursuing pleasure, he was filled with compassion;

When he saw how they lived in an age of wars, killing and wounding each other and since he knew that, on account of the fierce hate that raged in their hearts they were doomed to pay endless retribution, he was filled with compassion;

Since many who were born during the time of his Incarnation had heard him preaching the Holy Law, yet could not accept it, he was filled with compassion;

Since some possessed great fortunes which they were incapable of giving away, he was filled with compassion;

Since he saw the people of the world ploughing their fields, sowing the seed, doing business, haggling, buying and selling, to gain in the end nothing but bitterness, he was filled with compassion.

SUGGESTIONS FOR FURTHER READING

Conze, E., *Buddhist Scriptures*, Penguin
Appleton, G., *On the Eightfold Path*, SCM Press
Beswick, E., *Jataka Tales*, Murray
Percheron, M., *Buddha and Buddhism*, Longmans

4

SHINTOISM

SHINTOISM, THE original religion of Japan, is more alien
to us than Buddhism which it preceded. To the Westerner it
appears a primitive and bizarre religious doctrine, the outward
manifestations of which are the cult of nature and of ancestors.
There is no sharply distinguishing line between gods and men.
Shintoism knows three forms of ancestor worship: first, the
worship of personal ancestors, performed exclusively within
the closed family circle; second, the worship of certain 'clan'
gods; and third, the national-ancestor worship which consists
of the worship of the ancestors of the imperial family. To outsiders this last has always been the general characteristic of
Shintoism. The Mikados (this title is no longer used, having
been replaced by the name Tenno, 'heavenly king') are regarded
as the descendants of the sun-goddess Amaterasu Omi-kami
(the heaven-illumining goddess), whose heavenly grandson was
Ni-ni-gi-no-Mikoto. The great-grandson of the latter, Jimmu
Tenno, is said to have been the founder of the Japanese Empire
and the first (human) emperor, the founder of the dynasty
which has ruled Japan without interruption up to the present
day. The traditional date of foundation is 660 B.C. The present
emperor Tenno Heika, that is, His Majesty the Emperor (the
personal name Hirohito is no longer used), is the hundred and
twenty-fourth emperor since the first emperor Jimmu. In
our day, however, following Japan's defeat in the second World
War, Hirohito abolished the myth and, under a certain pressure
on the part of the American occupation authorities under the
late General MacArthur, made the solemn declaration that he
was not of divine origin. This sudden break with a centuries-
old tradition was expected to provoke a dangerous reaction on
the part of the populace, but this reaction was not forth-

coming. Hirohito now lives as a temporal ruler in the midst of his subjects and the so-called state Shintoism has disappeared.[1]

Shinto has been practised since time immemorial in the Land of the Rising Sun. It is anchored in the Japanese religious mentality and, though strongly influenced by Buddhism and Confucianism, it is inherent in the Japanese spirit and was never completely ousted by either of the above-mentioned beliefs.

Shinto (*Kami no Michi*) to use the classical name, means 'the Way of the Gods'. The word *Kami* (meaning 'above') must here be understood as *exalted*, holy, touched by the divine. Any object or being that gives rise to an emotion commands respect and can thus be considered as *Kami*. *Michi* is 'way'. However, the fact that in worldly life a person higher on the social scale can be referred to as *Kami* has led many to regard Shintoism more as a relationship between human beings than between God and man. In Shinto a man of noble character can be venerated as an exalted, divine being. In contrast with the religions of the theocratic type Shinto accepts the divine in the human. All that is 'higher' or more exalted in any respect is *Kami* and is venerated in Shinto.

In order not to become too involved in the complex of sects and trends we have contented ourselves with dividing Shinto into two classes: 'Sect Shinto', with its thirteen sects, and 'State Shinto' which has – outwardly at least, in its official form – been abolished. Each of the thirteen Shinto sects has its supporters; they are rumoured to number more than twenty-one million. In its earliest origin Shintoism is a lower nature religion or animism whereby a soul, sometimes even the power of speech, is attributed to trees, plants, flowers, seas and rocks. The early Japanese were surrounded on all sides by countless superhuman, supernatural and divine objects, organic and inorganic. Among the inorganic deified objects were celestial phenomena such as the sun and the moon, which were revered

---

[1] It will be remembered that America's policy with regard to defeated Japan came in for serious criticism. This led to conflicts which resulted in the recall of the late General MacArthur. The publicist M. Gain has written an interesting account of all this in *A Severe American Criticism of the Allied Occupation* (1948).

as chief gods: the sun goddess Amaterasu-Omi-kami and the moon god Tsu Kiyomi-no-Mikoto. Among the atmospheric phenomena the wind, heavy rains accompanied by storms, thunder and lightning all possessed a divine form. The seas, rivers and springs were the deified earthly phenomena.

Regarding the organic creatures, snakes, tigers, wolves and wild bears were the objects of 'zoolatry', the worship of animals, while 'dendrolatry', the worship of trees, also embraced grasses and grains. Miraculous virtues were, for example, attributed to peaches, especially in cases of necromancy. Primitive Shinto, moreover, worshipped various objects as idols: jewels, mirrors, swords and neckerchiefs. Dr Genchi Kato, the greatest modern authority on Shintoism, who has written a number of comprehensive works, speaks of various stages in the development of this religion.

From the primitive animistic phase, which might be characterized as 'polydemonic', Shinto evolved into 'polytheism' in the strictest sense of the word. A clear differentiation developed between gods and goddesses: father, mother, husband and wife, brother and sister, master and servant made their entry into the circle of gods, exactly as in human society. It was possible to speak of a divine hierarchy. The family relationships were even clearly defined: Su-sa-no-wo-no-Mikoto, the deified storm with lashing rains, was a brother of the sun goddess Amaterasu-Omi-kami. Together with Tsu Kiyomi-no-Mikoto, the moon god, they were born of the divine parents Izanagi and Izanami. They reigned respectively over the Plane of the High Heavens, over the wide expanse of the Ocean and over the Kingdom of the Night. As often happens in human families, this family of gods was also divided by quarrels and discord, chiefly between the sun goddess and her brother. The sun goddess was victorious and Su-sa-no-wo was banished by order of the eighty myriad gods (or 'countless gods') who assembled in the dry bed of 'the (Sacred) River of the Heavens', the Milky Way. Here one finds some resemblance to Greek mythology in which a council of the gods met on the summit of Olympus, presided over by Zeus with his consort Hera, his son Apollo, his daughter Athene and other divine dignitaries. But Su-sa-no-wo refused to be cowed and fought back so forcefully and so mercilessly against his sister that Amaterasu was obliged to take refuge in a heavenly cave, thus plunging heaven and earth into pitchy darkness. Once again the eighty myriad gods met to consult together, and succeeded in persuading the sun goddess to leave her hiding place and to illumine the universe once again. Her brother was banished from heaven to earth. He landed in the province of Izumo (Western Japan), and married the daughter of a local deity. Their union produced the celebrated Okuninushi-no-Kami, the Great Divine Lord of this region, whose remains are venerated as a sacred relic at Kitsuki.

It was Ni-ni-go-no-Mikoto, the grandson of the sun goddess Amaterasu, who received from his heavenly grandmother the command to rule over Japan. 'May our imperial race be continued prosperous and uninterrupted,' she said, 'existing for ever together with Heaven and Earth.' This was the beginning of the worship of the emperors and their ancestors. The Western reader will be struck by the parallel with the Old Testament when the Lord tells Abraham to go to the land that he will show him. 'To your descendants I will give this land' (Gen. 12.1-8).

It is hard to realize that the pantheon of Shinto gods numbers a hundred thousand divinities, worshipped in 196,000 temples and sanctuaries. The central place of worship is the Daidzjingo at Isé, dedicated to the sun goddess Amaterasu. The sanctuary is rebuilt unchanged every twenty years to preserve it from decay. It contains two rooms, and the rear chamber may never be entered since it is the resting place of the goddess's mortal remains, so wrapped up as to be concealed even from the eye of the initiates. There are no statues but *shintai*, objects 'in which part of the essence of a *kami* has lodged'. The *shintai* of the sun goddess is a sacred metal mirror, which is part of the regalia of the imperial family, symbolizing both the divinity and the temporal power of the emperors.

As a rule the ordinary temples are made of wood, left in its natural state, with a straw roof. The ritual acts are performed in a special hall, and the visitor may take part after he has drawn the deity's attention to his presence by means of a gong. Divine protection is sought against all sorts of evils, sicknesses, earthquakes, floods and typhoon. The magical songs of the priests form part of the ritual activities. There are 16,000 of these, spread over the entire country. Japan comprises more than four thousand islands of which only five hundred are inhabited. The temple may only be entered in a state of physical cleanliness and spiritual purity. The old ritual prayers are recited by priests, not to the people but to a particular deity. Plastic representations of the gods are unknown, with the exception of the goddess of happiness Oezume, the phallic god Sarutahiko, Inari the goddess of the rice, and Ebisue the protective deity of fishermen and merchants. These gods, however, are never worshipped in the temple.

In his chapter on the religions of Japan,[2] Professor C. C. Krieger writes: 'In the months of July and August thousands of pilgrims climb the most beautiful of Japan's mountains, the sacred Fujiyama.[3] Having spent the night in the eighth of the ten rest stations, they hope to behold the great light in the early morning. And so, too, in towns and villages throughout the country, tens of thousands of Japanese attempt to attract the attention of Asahi, the Rising Sun, by clapping their hands. But there are also mountains, often labelled male or female according to their shape, rocks, waterfalls, rivers and strangely shaped or age-old trees which may be considered as *kami*.' And he continues: 'From time immemorial prayers have been offered to the gods of wind and rain, sea, fire and earth, to the phallic gods which dwell in representations of phalluses erected along the roadside, and also to animals which are regarded as the mounts of the gods. Sacrifice is also made to them in order to gain their favour. These sacrifices consist of rice, fruit, fish, vegetables and *sake*, the holy wine fermented from rice, and on some occasions of textile products.'

The veneration of the deceased which occupies such an important place in Shinto deserves particular attention. In personal ancestor worship the souls of the deceased are repre-

---

[2] *De Godsdiensten der Wereld* (World Religions) (third impression) edited by Professor C. J. Bleeker.

[3] This is how Professor Krieger writes the name of this mountain but, as we are informed by reliable sources, this version is not correct. It should be Fuji-no-jama or Fuji-san.

sented as small planks which are placed upon the household altar. To these daily offerings in the form of rice, fish, incense and flowers are made on rising and before retiring. It is curious to recall that we Westerners, too, are often accustomed to place flowers before the portrait of a deceased loved one as a significant mark of love and respect.

When a practising Shintoist dies, his remains, after having been laid out, are placed in a coffin. Into the coffin too go a number of objects which the deceased was accustomed to use during his lifetime (a sword or fan). During the memorial service the Shinto priest invites the soul to take up its abode in 'the house of the exalted soul', a sober wooden cupboard containing a small white plank on which is written the name, age and date of death of the deceased. This cupboard with the soul which has now become *kami* are preserved in the family of the dead person after the mortal remains have been laid to rest.

The attitude to the clan gods, the tutelary deities of villages and small communities, was formerly of an emotional nature. They watched over the houses and their protection extended no further than the native inhabitants of these villages or communities. They alleviated the lot of these people and it is thus understandable that shortly after the birth of their children the parents hastened to the temple to have the baby blessed by the priest. We are dealing here with a sort of ancestor worship, for each tribe had its ancestor as tutelary god, except for the prominent families which had chosen one of the nature gods. For many centuries these prominent families possessed unrivalled power in Japan. They occupied the highest positions, which they declared to be hereditary, and carried on among themselves a merciless struggle for power. The families of Mononobe and Soga became renowned in Japanese history, but they literally exterminated each other. Later came the Fujiwara, the Minamoto and the Hodjo families, in whose hands the emperor was a complaisant tool, although he continued to be worshipped as a deity. As early as the ninth century the emperors lost their effective power, which was usurped by members of the Fujiwara family. In 1192 Minamoto Joritomo acquired the title *shogun* (literally 'supreme commander') and became the actual ruler of Japan. Since then three so-called *shogunates* have held power. During this period of Japanese history the emperor and his court led a shadowy existence in Kyoto. The emperors retained no real power but always remained 'spiritual heads of the nation'. In 1868 the power of the *shoguns* came to an end, and executive authority was restored to the royal family, which had received its commission from the sun goddess Amaterasu in the dawn of Japanese history. About ten years before, Japan's isolation had come to an end with the establishment of relations with the great powers and with the opening up of the country to foreign trade. All this, however, was not accomplished without bloody and violent incidents.

Meanwhile the introduction of new ideas into Japan from the continent of Asia had profoundly affected Shintoism, which had evolved both ethically and intellectually. It had passed from polytheism to a form of henotheism which promotes belief in one particular god (in this case the sun goddess Amaterasu) without denying the existence of other gods. In the Kogosjoi (literally: *Gleanings from Old Tales*) which have been translated into English, it is said: 'Since Amaterasu-Omi-kami is the greatest ancestral goddess, no Shinto god can lay claim to equality, just as no son is ever equal to his father or a vassal to his Lord.' Amaterasu is exalted above every other God, her existence is not material but purely spiritual, therefore she must be worshipped in the spirit. Hence any portrayal of the gods is rejected. If we attempt to establish a relationship between the deity and man by means of a representation, this image will stand in its own way and hinder us from attaining our religious goal: direct communion with the deity. An image made by mortal hands is of no value in the Shinto-teaching.'

Whereas in old Shinto physical, not spiritual, purity was one of the fundamental religious laws, as the religion grew more 'intellectual' greater emphasis was laid upon inner purity, cleanness of heart. 'To do good is to be pure, to do evil is to be impure; the gods abhor evil deeds because these are impure.' It is also laid down that there are two meanings of purity: outward or physical purity and inward purity. The truly upright man can be sure of attaining communion with the divine. This is nothing other than inward purity or integrity, which is the same as purity or uprightness of heart. This in turn came to mean that people of moral nobility could be 'canon-ized'. This has happened in our day with the famous General Maresoeke Nogi who had been governor of Formosa but had gained great laurels during the Russo-Japanese war by the conquest of Port Arthur. On the death of Emperor Moetsuhito in 1912 he and his wife committed *hara-kiri* (suicide) from a spirit of devotion to their sovereign. A Shinto altar or shrine is dedicated to him in the neighbour-hood of Tokyo. Emperor Moetsuhito himself is venerated in a temple at Jojogi, a part of Tokyo. This temple is second in importance to the Daidzjingo at Isé where the sun goddess Amaterasu is honoured. Even during Moetsuhito's lifetime holy places were set up in his honour, in the village of Ono in the province of Shinano, in the port of Istunomaki and at Koesatu-Matshi which forms part of Hiroshima.

Until 1 January 1946, the Japanese emperor was a visible deity; 'mikadoism', emperor-worship, formed part of the religion. It is remarkable now, after all that has happened in Japan since the end of the second World War, to read in the already mentioned book by Genchi Kato, which dates from 1935, that the religious belief and national consciousness of the Japanese people are so closely interwoven as to be in-separable. Shinto, which is characterized as a belief in the divinity of the ruler, is not, according to Kato, a doctrine subsequently accepted by the state as the state religion, but a religion which lives *a priori* in the heart of every Japanese. This is why a Japanese never ceases to be a Shintoist. When, in addition, Kato goes on to say that 'the abjuration of the national Shinto religion would be tantamount to treason against the Empire and disloyalty towards its divine ruler', one is all the more amazed that Emperor Hirohito's renun-ciation of his supposed divine origin and the abolition of Shinto as the state religion provoked such little reaction. Can it be that the pillars upon which popular belief in Japan rested had mouldered away during the course of the centuries and had partly decayed?

According to tradition, Buddhism reached China from India in 67 A.D. This date is accepted on the strength of a dream which the Chinese emperor, Ming-ti, is supposed to have had, in which he was commanded to disseminate Buddhism throughout his empire. It is thought possible that even before this time independent Buddhist communities already existed in West China, although hitherto Confucianism had predominated at the imperial court.

Chinese Buddhism, however, diverges in important points from the Indian. Centuries of evolution had transformed it into an entirely distinct religion, completely adapted to the nature of the Chinese people with their astonishingly rich cultural life, their philosophy and artistic sense, often coupled with a primitive superstition and barbaric delusions. It was not until the eighth century that the evolutionary process was completed and it gained a firm foothold. Only one sect of any significance was not of Chinese origin but imported directly from India. It was called *Shen-yen* (the true word) or *Mi-chaou* (the secret teaching) but its influence was slight. This was also the case with a number of smaller sects based on Indian Buddhism which later reached Japan. They either disappeared or survived as purely historical relics.

Around 550 Buddhism, in its Mahayana form, entered Japan by way of Korea. At this time one of the kings of the Korean countries sent envoys to Japan with gifts for the reigning Emperor Kimmei, insisting, however, that he should be converted to Buddhism. The emperor ordered one of his ministers, Soga no Iname, to test the Korean Buddha statue by venerating it. Soga, who had been gripped by the new doctrine, erected a sanctuary in his home which soon attracted a crowd of interested visitors. Naturally enough all this provoked violent opposition in the Shintoist court circles, but they were obliged to admit defeat when it appeared that the emperor was a convert to the new faith. It was during the reign of Shotoku (in 593) that Buddhism was elevated to a state religion. From then onwards a succession of Korean priests and temple builders crossed over to Japan, encouraged by prince-regent Oemayado, who had a 'constitution' of seventeen articles drawn up which established the system of government and stipulated a state morality, having as its aim, among other things, the promotion of the Buddhist religion. 'Cease from desiring and cast aside

your wishes,' said one of the articles. Oemayado was a convinced Buddhist who held meetings in his palace in order to
explain the Buddhist doctrine personally. He also conducted
frequent religious ceremonies in the temples. He founded a
Buddhist Institute in the neighbourhood of Osaka for the study
of Buddhist philosophy, and maintained a close spiritual contact with China, to which he sent monks and teachers as well
as political envoys.

The Korean culture of the period was very strongly influenced by Buddhism. It was the Koreans in the first instance
who introduced the Japanese to Buddhist philosophy and religion as well as to Buddhist art. Many temples in and around
Nara (the capital of Japan from 710 to 784) bear elequent
testimony to this. Soon, however, Japan turned directly to
China for instruction. Although Japan originally adopted
Chinese Buddhism in a practically unaltered form, she finally
imparted to it a completely distinctive character. In our search
through the works on Japanese Buddhism we found that Sir
Charles Eliot mentions as the most striking characteristic of this
Buddhism the fact that it was clearly adapted to both the
political and social conditions of the country. It proved extremely sensitive to sudden political changes, reflecting them,
as it were, in its sects which in their turn expressed the special
aspects in their art.[4]

Although Buddhism exercised an enormous missionary force,
it did not succeed in replacing Shintoism. The native religion
maintained its position not only because it had such a firm hold
on the Japanese mind but also thanks to the natural tolerance
of Buddhism. After a period of unmistakable hostility a compromise was reached which has become known as Rioboe-
Shinto or Bipartite Shinto. The Shinto gods were regarded as
temporary manifestations of the Buddhist gods whose true land
of origin was India but who had left behind their tokens on
passing through Japan. They were recognized as incarnations
of Buddha or of Bodhisattvas (Buddhas-to-be) and the temples
– with the exception of the temple at Isé, dedicated to the sun
goddess Amaterasu and a number of other holy places – were

---

[4] We are indebted, for a number of important facts, to Sir
Charles Eliot's work, *Japanese Buddhism*.

handed over to Buddhist priests. In this way Shinto was to some extent absorbed by Buddhism but possessed sufficient vital force to be ready to emerge on every occasion for which it received official sanction, even in periods when it seemed completely outstripped by new trends of thought. One might sum up the contrast between Shintoism and Buddhism thus: Shinto is the expression of the fundamental ideas regarding family and national life. This is both its strength and its weakness. It expresses the most personal and the most vital concepts of the Japanese people. Buddhism, on the other hand, gave even more. It developed and refined the national character but did not reflect the national ideals although it adapted itself to them. 'A Japanese may believe anything he likes provided his faith is not in conflict with the institutions of his country.'

We shall take the liberty here of quoting a number of remarks from the introduction to Sir Charles Eliot's work, *Japanese Buddhism*. There was, in his view, a 'constant tendency to separate titular and real power. . . . Not only was the Government administered during long periods by *shoguns* who rendered merely ceremonial homage to the Emperor, but the authority of the *shogun* sometimes passed into the hands of a deputy, and at other times the real power was in the hands of an ex-Emperor who had nominally abdicated.' The other noteworthy feature was 'the remarkable attitude towards foreigners. Japan appears throughout the ages to have been the most assimilative of all nations and the most anxious to borrow from others, and yet the most deliberately self-secluded and anxious to avoid contact with all without. The wholesale adoption of Buddhism and of Chinese culture in the sixth century was the work of individuals rather than the result of international intercourse, and after about 850 such intercourse altogether ceased. . . . When Christianity arrived from the West the Japanese were at first perfectly friendly, and imitation of Christian customs was for a moment fashionable, but as soon as political consequences were suspected, Europeans, with the exception of a few Dutch, were expelled and Christianity was forbidden.'

The political phases of development through which Japan

D

passed can be summed up as follows: before the fifth century
A.D. the student is more concerned with archaeology than with
history. Authentic records only made their appearance with
the coming of Buddhism and the Chinese civilization. In 645
the growth of the Chinese influence culminated in a sudden and
complete administrative revolution; the entire government was
reformed to correspond with the Chinese bureaucratic system.
In 793 the capital was transferred from Nara to Kyoto. The
emperors tended increasingly to withdraw from public life, and
from 826 to 1050 the actual political power was in the hands
of the Fujiwara family. This long rule ended in the eleventh
century when the Houses of Taira and Minamoto came into
prominence and began a struggle for power. The latter family
won and Joritomo, the head of the Minamotos, received from
the emperor the title of *shogun*. In 1854 Japan was opened up
to relations with the outside world at the insistence of the
United States. Between 1641 and 1854 the Chinese and the
Dutch were the only foreigners permitted to trade with Japan.

At the restoration of 1868, when the emperor regained his
full powers, Shinto was also restored (for a time) as state
religion. Although the Constitution of 1889 guaranteed freedom
of religion to the Japanese, every Japanese was none the less
expected, as a loyal subject, to accept certain tenets of the
Shinto doctrine. School children had to visit Shinto temples at
appointed times (national feast-days, for example). The authorities decreed that the Shinto mythology should be treated and
taught as the official early history of Japan. After the capitula-
tion of 1945, however, State Shinto was almost immediately
banned by the occupying forces.

This introductory summary has brought us to the heart of our
dissertation: the essence of Japanese Buddhism.[5] It is derived
from the Mahayana. In our chapter on the origin of Buddhism
in India we have already pointed out the difference between the
Hinayana, the southern form of Buddhism, and the *Mahayana*,
the northern Buddhism. The first is the small, lesser path, or

[5] On this subject we consulted Professor M. W. de Visser's book,
Buddha's Leer in het Verre Oosten (Buddha's Teaching in the Far
East).

the 'Little Vehicle', the second the greater, better path, or 'Great Vehicle' (see above, pp. 74 ff.).

In the beginning of the ninth century two important mystical sects were founded by Dengyo Daishi and Kobo Daishi: the sect of Tendai (which derives its name from the mountain T'ien-t'ai in China where it had its headquarters) and Shingon, the Sino-Japanese rendering of the Chinese Shen-yen (the true word), a school introduced from India by way of China. Dengyo Daishi was renowned for his great knowledge of the mystical rituals and was one of the most perfect exponents of meditation. Kobo Daishi acquired considerable knowledge from his extensive travels and was, moreover, a poet and calligrapher. Both feared that the priesthood would become too worldly in the great cities and soon fled from the cities to devote themselves to study in solitude. Dengyo became the founder of an extensive monastic settlement near Kyoto and Kobo of a monastery which expanded into a temple complex of about 1,200 buildings. Their philosophical labours led to the spread of Buddhism among the lower classes and to the merging of Shinto and Buddhism in the afore-mentioned Rioboe-Shinto.

The number of Buddhas who preach their doctrine in an unbounded succession of worlds is infinite. 'For probably no nation in the world,' says Professor M. W. de Visser, 'possessed such a deep insight into the immensity of the universe and of time as the ancient Indians.' The historical Buddha differs noticeably from the Buddha of the Mahayana as practised in China, Japan and also in Central Asia and Indonesia. He is not the exalted human being who is venerated as a saint, but a divine Buddha seated between two Bodhi-sattvas (Buddhas-to-be) who represent Universal Goodness. The first is enthroned upon a lotus cushion upon the back of the sacred white elephant, while the second sits with legs crossed upon a lion and drives away all evil spirits. He possesses a number of supernatural qualities which elevate him above humanity and – as we already indicated in our chapter on Buddhism – has various bodies: the Truth-Body which is out-wardly invisible, only becoming visible to the eye of the spirit in deep meditation, the Enjoyment- (or Bliss-)body which dwells in Paradise and sometimes manifests itself in heavenly form to the most devout of the dying, and the Transformation-body, the human form in which he appears on earth in order to preach the doctrine and to redeem living creatures.

In Japan, during the course of the centuries, the historical Buddha faded increasingly into the background, to be replaced by the Truth-Body, the heavenly Buddha known as Amida. Yet, like the original Indian Buddhism, Japanese Buddhism has four places of pilgrimage, dedicated to the historical Buddha. Buddha is worshipped here as a new-born child, as an ascetic preacher, as the possessor of the highest wisdom and as the deceased. Particularly fascinating is the image of Amida or Amitabha, the celestial Buddha who is always ready to receive the souls of all who pray to him with true faith in their hearts. 'Even the most hardened sinner finds grace in his eyes if, in his last moments, the light which radiates from Buddha's face pierces his heart.' He symbolizes the setting sun, to whom prayers are directed when the hereafter is in question. Amida is accompanied by two Bodhisattvas: Kwannon ('the Lord who is seen'), who embodies the infinite compassion of Amida, and Seishi ('He who has attained the great station'), who hands on Amida's wisdom. The Amida school, which originated towards the end of the twelfth century, is frequently called the 'easy path' because one relies on the strength of another, in this case Amida, instead of upon one's own virtue and repentance. This is in contrast to the 'Noble Eightfold Path' towards Nirvana of the historical Buddha (see above, pp. 68 ff.). The Amida school led to the founding of various sects, in the first place the Yuzu-nembutsu or sect of the deeply penetrating Prayer (which still exists and comprises three hundred and fifty-five temples and monasteries and more than six hundred chapels), followed by the sect of the Pure Land from which in turn emerged the True Sect of the Pure Land. Finally there is the *Shi-sho*, the Sect of Times, so-called because it prescribes a prayer to Amida six times a day. All these sects exercised some influence and several of them were very powerful for a considerable period.

Later wise men made the faith more democratic, with the result that the lower classes, too, were soon producing preachers.

The most celebrated of these was Nichiren (the Sun-Lotus). He lived from 1222 to 1282 and had a strong grip on the masses through the force of his words and his inexhaustible knowledge. He was born in Kominato, a small fishing village, which still honours his memory with a temple. Nichiren was eleven years old when he was sent by his father to a neighbouring monastery, where he was ordained four years later. As his knowledge increased he began to be troubled by doubts concerning the purity of Japanese Buddhism. He proposed to restore its original purity and unity. He visited a number of places and spent ten years in Hieisan, the great religious centre of the day, where he came to the conclusion that the so-called Tendai teaching, as preached by Dengyo Daishi (which implied the recognition of the Lotus as the centre of Truth yet permitted the worship of Amida, the celestial Buddha), was the correct doctrine provided it was presented in a form adapted to the times. On 17 May 1253 he proclaimed a new doctrine, summed up as 'homage to the *sutra* of the Lotus of the Good Law'. He propagated his views, however, in such a violent manner, jeering at those whose opinion differed from his, that no monastery would keep him for any length of time. He wandered about for quite a long time, even built a small dwelling in the neighbourhood of Kamakura and soon made a name for himself as a travelling preacher. These were troubled times, with earthquakes, plague epidemics and famines, while political quarrels and conspiracies undermined the state. It was at this period that he wrote his Treatise on the Justice and the Safety of the State in which he testified to his belief in the eternal teaching of the historical Buddha whose life is revealed in man. Man can become aware of this revelation by adoring the perfect truth in sincere surrender and by attempting to attain perfection by means of lofty thoughts and moral behaviour. The document was composed in the form of a dialogue between the master and a visitor who came to discuss with him 'the signs of the times'.

Concerning the chief trends of this document Eliot says that it identified religion and national life: they are one. Another striking feature is its boundless intolerance. The killing of heretics is not regarded as murder and it is the government's task to exterminate heresy with the sword. The sect of the Pure Land was unconditionally condemned since it denied man's powerlessness to attain his own salvation, rejected the celibacy of the priests and abstention from meat and fish, but regarded social work as a means of attaining bliss.

The government was considerably startled at receiving such a 'memorandum'; the clergy roused the people against Nichiren, who was finally banished to the lonely coast of the peninsula of Izo. He did not remain there long but returned to his monastery in Kamakura and took up his studies and struggle again. Soon a new work of his appeared: questions and answers concerning man's attitude towards the Lotus of Truth. This volume was even more violent and more aggressive than the first, so that even his supporters were relieved when Nichiren departed for four years in order to carry on his missionary work in the Eastern provinces. None the less, his attacks on 'Church and State' did not decrease in violence; he wrote letters to the authorities in which he warned against a Mongol invasion and explained that the only way to save the country was to accept his teaching as the State religion. It seemed impossible to stop Nichiren's flow of testimony. Once again he was imprisoned and condemned to death, but the execution did not take place and he was banished to the island of Sado in the sea of Japan. Here he spent two years under extremely harsh conditions, which did not, however, prevent him from devoting himself to further meditation or from writing a great number of treatises. One of these was entitled Kaimo-Koesho, 'the opening of the eyes', in which he repeated his firm determination to continue working for the establishment of the Truth. He took three vows: 'I will be the mainstay of Japan'; 'I will be the eyes of Japan'; 'I will be the "great ship of Japan"' (in other words, the giver of life). He identified himself with the Bodhisattva who was charged by the historical Buddha with the defence and propagation of the faith.

And still there was no end to his activities. In vain the government tried to get him to compromise with other sects. He was deaf to all proposals but the unity of Japan under Buddhism as he understood it: the founding of a central Buddhist Church which would one day rule the world. Meanwhile his prestige had grown considerably as a result of the Mongol invasions which he had predicted. He founded the temples of Minobu and Ikegami which are still the holy places of the members of his sect. He died in 1282, and it is typical of the influence of his personality, which is at the same time historical and legendary, that even in our day, as recently as 1922, a spiritual title has been conferred upon him. He left behind him a powerful sect under the leadership of six of his best disciples.

In the period which followed the opening up of Japan to foreign trade, which resulted in a rapid orientation towards the West, the country developed into a military power of the first rank. The urge to expand, the conquests on the continents of Asia and the penetration in Korea were a source of worry to the United States and the Western powers for many years. The 'yellow peril' was no illusion, as was shatteringly proved by the second World War. The search for *'lebensraum'* by the Land of the Rising Sun, with its centuries-old civilization yet brand new materialism, was understandable but difficult to reconcile with the oriental wisdom and meekness preached by Shinto Buddhism. Modern Japan possessed a dynamic and militaristic drive which was frequently regarded as 'Prussian' by the West, but which soon proved to contain the much more dangerous and criminal elements of Hitlerism. The years 1942-45 brought home to many unfortunates that there was little to choose between the 'Jap' and the 'Nazi'.

Some of those who are familiar with the Orient seem to think that Zen Buddhism, which came into prominence in Japan when the military class acquired its predominating influence, contained the seeds of the Japanese mentality as we have come to know it today. This may sound strange, for the Zen sect, which came to China in 512 and entered Japan around 1200, would by then have been already seven centuries old before it exerted an evil influence upon the modern Japanese mentality. And yet it is impossible to dismiss this notion out of hand. Zen Buddhism, after all, was intended to train the ruling class in spiritual strength and steadfastness, a mental discipline which sought absolute truth outside the concepts of good and evil. It taught its adepts to bear pain stoically, to despise death, to realize the insignificance of earthly life. To the disciples of Zen Buddhism parting from this world comes easily.

Bushido, 'the Way of the Warrior', a code of honour which in feudal times had developed naturally in the warrior class and contained both Confucian elements and views derived from Zen, was artificially revived in modern times by the authorities. In addition, a sort of link with Shinto was propagated. The military code of the modern Japanese army was thus in fact based upon a combination of the Shinto ideas concerning their being a 'chosen people, ruled by an emperor of divine origin', and a system of ethics belonging to a long vanished feudal age. The soldier going into battle severed all ties with life and placed himself unconditionally at the service of an idea: the unification of all Asiatic peoples under the leadership of the Tenno, emperor. We have seen whither this 'Way of the Warrior' has led in our day.

However, it would be unfair to the deeper significance of Zen Buddhism to judge it solely by this manifestation. *Zen* is short for *Zen-na* and reflects one of the central concepts of Mahayana Buddhism: the believer is so lost in inner meditation that his thoughts are turned away from the world of phenomena and become freed of all desire and self-seeking. The general meaning of Zen is meditation and contemplative life. The Zen Buddhist derives his insight into life not from a saviour but from his own mental powers. He is little attracted to dogmas and ceremonies, and attributes no exclusive authority to the written word. For him the most important thing is to penetrate to the nature of life and death and to realize that 'our own heart is Buddha himself'.

The spread of such a meditative doctrine as Zen among the military class becomes understandable when one takes into account the fact that it possesses no elaborate philosophy and emphasizes the sharing in the Truth which comes to man as a vision through introspection and not through the study of another's words. Most warriors were not sufficiently developed intellectually to understand the complicated terminology of other sects. The sudden intuition, which is called *satori* and which is the goal of the Zen Buddhist, is an inner, personal experience. A Zen teacher reads no *sutras* (doctrines), performs no ceremonies and venerates no images. He instructs his pupils not by means of long sermons but by helpful suggestions. The disciple must examine himself, learn self-control and find his place in the spiritual universe through his own efforts. Zen is so little 'communicative' that it possesses no canon. Its earliest literature, although very extensive, consists for the most part of biographical details concerning the teachers and collections of questions used for 'testing' the pupil. The masters spoke as obscurely as possible, often in paradoxes which were sometimes accompanied by slaps or ear-splitting cries which were intended to confuse the pupil.

It is clear that a system like this, without dogmas, was capable of attracting a fairly varied range of supporters. At the outset Zen encountered considerable opposition from other sects, which called it an arrogant mysticism which encouraged eccentricity. Time has shown, however, that Zen Buddhism, despite a tinge of charlatanism, has brought the Japanese people both aesthetic and spiritual uplift.

The founder of Zen Buddhism is generally considered to be the Indian monk, Patriarch Bodhiharma, who appeared in China from India around A.D. 520. He originally found a supporter in Wo-ti, the first emperor of the Liang dynasty. Wo-ti was a Confucianist who later became an ardent Buddhist. He gave public explanations of the Buddhist writings and for three short periods became a monk in order to propagate the doctrine among the people. Although his reign lasted for more than forty-seven years, in the end he fell into disfavour with his people, probably because of his secret understanding with apostate religious groups. He lost both his kingdom and his life. It was under his auspices that the first edition of the Chinese *Tripitaka* (or *Tipitaka*) saw the light. This is thought to have contained about 2,200 works, including travel stories. He sent a mission to Magadha to acquire certain Sanskrit texts. On returning home his emissaries brought with them not only the precious manuscripts but also the scholarly translator Paramartha, whom they persuaded to settle in China.

Bodhidharma, who is thought to have been the son of a regional king in southern India, was living in Canton when he was invited to Nanking by the Emperor Wo-ti. The first contacts were fruitful, but when Bodhidharma roundly informed the emperor that his majesty did not sufficiently appreciate the essential value of the faith and that there was no merit in building temples and in having writings translated into Chinese, since there is only one truth, born of the revelation of Buddha, the emperor's enthusiasm cooled somewhat. It was not long before Bodhidharma left Nanking and returned to an isolated temple with the firm intention of avoiding henceforth the company of princes and the higher clergy. In his *Japanese Buddhism* Sir Charles Eliot mentions a legend according to which Bodhidharma sat for nine years on a wall, staring in front of him, until finally both his legs fell off. The legend is perpetuated in a legless doll with which many Japanese children still play today.

Zen Buddhism was introduced into Japan in 1202 by the Japanese master Eisai. Eisai made several trips to China where the Zen philosophy had many supporters at that period. He studied it and introduced it to Japan on his return. This was not the first time the Japanese had encountered Zen Buddhism. It had made an appearance in Japan between 615 and 815 together with many other Chinese sects, but it made no impression and died out. It was only accepted with the coming of Eisai, but has since become so fused with Japanese life that it is regarded as the most specifically Japanese of all forms of Buddhism.

In addition to Eisai's other merits, which were considerable, there is one thing for which the Japanese must be eternally grateful to him: he succeeded in transforming tea drinking into a national rite. We cannot resist the temptation to diverge a moment from our subject proper in order to consider the institution of the *Cha-no-jo*, which, literally translated, means 'Hot water of (from) tea'. Professor C. C. Krieger had this to say of it: 'Although according to Chinese and Japanese sources it (the tea ceremony) gradually came into fashion in South China as a means of combating the priests' sleepiness during meditation exercises in the Zen monasteries, its origin is probably much older. Introduced into Japan by Eisai during the Kamakura period (1192-1333), it acquired a more profane character in the fifteenth century under the Ashkaga *shoguns*, involving considerable luxury and the spending of fortunes.'⁶ He goes on to say: 'The chief aim of the ceremony is to rid the tired and confused mind of cares and difficulties, to confer strength upon the exponent for tranquil meditation and to help to restore his feeling of harmony with nature.' The institution of Cha-no-jo is constructed upon elements of Zen and has found its way into all the educated circles of Japan, where it has played a great part in forming taste and custom.

The cult of communal tea-drinking finds its adepts among soldiers, statesmen and merchants, doctors, lawyers and artists. It is even taught as a subject in the girls' secondary schools as part of the training in good manners. Without a knowledge of Cha-no-jo, one would not feel at ease in cultivated Japanese circles, says Professor Krieger, and without a knowledge of the spirit behind it one could not understand Japanese art: it finds expression in the architecture of temples and dwelling houses, in the art of furnishing, landscape gardening and flower arrangement. It forms a beautiful custom in daily life and it teaches an appreciation of beauty in one's own actions and in those of others. Yet it is not purely aesthetic; it is closely linked with ethics and religion and aims at giving expression to man's relationship to nature. It signifies hygiene for it promotes cleanliness; it fosters economy, because it attempts to make its exponents feel at home in stark surroundings. 'We could consider it,' according to Professor Krieger, 'as the true characteristic of Japanese culture, rooted in an amalgam of elements taken from the two oldest civilizations of the East – India and China – and fashioned by the great tea-masters of Japan into a creation which has made material taste stronger, healthier and more sensitive.'

Zen Buddhism, with its simple, practical social system of ethics, its meekness and serenity on the one hand and its incitement to

⁶ 'Het Zen-Buddhism en zijn invloed op de geest van Japan' (Zen Buddhism and its Influence on the Mind of Japan), an inaugural address (1948).

military virtues on the other, appealed to the masses and penetrated all social strata. This gave rise to the dualism in the
spirit of the Japanese people which has persisted up to the
present day – artistic sensibility and simplicity combined with
aggressiveness. It remains surprising, however, that this contemplative and mystical doctrine, which one would have expected to flourish more among those who had retired from the
hostility of life, should have become the favourite code of the
military class. This is generally attributed to the fact that the
Zen truth is not found in any 'scripture' but is acquired through
the experience of the human mind. Zen is essentially discipline,
the mind is kept under control and does not allow itself to be
ensnared by physical danger from without or by passion from
within. It would be mistaken to assert that the modern Japanese
soldier is experienced in the philosophy of Zen, but it may be
said that *go*-masters, fencers and other sportsmen, for example,
are only considered to be properly trained when, besides the
required skill, they can also command the secret knowledge
entrusted by the teachers to their pupils. They must know, for
example, that the spirit must be 'free', i.e. clear, without prejudice and ready to follow every lofty inspiration.

A glaring contradiction in Zen Buddhism is that it has exercised a considerable influence upon various branches of art.
The monasteries provided teachers for education, renowned
statesmen and a large section of the civil service was recruited
from young men who had done their training in Zen monasteries.

Zen Buddhism in Japan has three clearly defined sects:
Rinzai, Soto and Obaku. The Soto sect is the largest and
emerged at the beginning of the thirteenth century, twenty-five
years after the Rinzai. The Obaku is of a later date, c. 1660,
and has adopted a large number of Chinese customs. All three
sects have the same doctrines, but different hierarchies. There
is, however, a difference in the method followed by the Soto
and the Rinzai sects. The first lays the emphasis on moral training and gradual development in order to obtain 'enlightenment'; the second postulates that this enlightenment is rather
a sudden revelation which cannot be attained or hastened by
study. There is a saying among Buddhists which compares

enlightenment with a mountain top which can be reached from all sides by various paths; each sect, however, insists that its own path is the best and shortest. This idea in any case is not confined to Buddhism; one often meets it nearer home, in the 'pillared' West.

The differences are small but the nuances great between the predominant sects in Japanese Buddhism – Tendai, Shingon, Amidism, Zen. They have, however, one thing in common. They have all contributed to a high degree to the refinement of cultural and artistic life. In this respect the so-called Kamakura period is of exceptional significance.

In the policy carried out by Minamoto Joritomo, the first *shogun* of the so-called Kamakura shogunate, one can still find traces of the earliest growth of institutions which survived for seven centuries and which, even after they had disappeared, left behind them an imprint which has still not been entirely effaced. Joritomo's primary aim was to acquire as much territory and as many supporters as possible. By ensuring an economic and military domination Japan would acquire great political force, though it is doubtful whether Joritomo and his immediate successors ever entertained any clear concept of national unity. They thought in general terms like feudal estates and lordships of the manor and not in concepts like people and government. Everything was directed towards the protection of individual personalities as the embodiment of the country's power and well-being. It is the warriors' task – so it was said – to be like the monk who follows an established teaching. It is his task to preserve the state by protecting the sovereign. Whether he possesses only a small piece of land or an extensive domain, his loyalty to his lord must be the same. He must regard his life not as his own but as a life offered to his lord and master. A son may sacrifice his parents in the interest of his supreme war lord, a husband may sell his wife to a house of ill-fame to obtain the necessary money in order to defend as a warrior the honour of his *shogun*. In the course of time this philosophy produced the harsh code of the military caste. In contrast to the European ideal of chivalry which developed in an atmosphere of religious inspiration, the Japanese feudal warrior, although he worshipped the god of war and venerated the Buddhist deities by inward instinct, was by no means filled with religious enthusiasm.

Yet it is a remarkable fact (and there is so much that is remarkable and incomprehensible to our Western way of thinking in the development of the religious life and in the social norms of the Japanese) that the deeds and ideas of the military class of those days were not entirely free from religious influence. During this Kamakura period both the feudal lords and the vassals founded Buddhist temples, and when a warrior returned from a campaign he entered a monastery and assumed a Buddhist name. Art and literature flourished, and architecture explored new forms. A number of monasteries were built, old temples were restored, sculptors were attracted from China, new schools arose in art, and new trends developed in literature.

It will always remain one of the most precious merits of religions that – no matter how they differ in their concept of the nature of the Supreme Being and in the cult which they advocate – they have throughout the ages, alongside their religious teaching and their philosophical systems, always inspired artists great and small to new creative efforts.

In the case of Japan the inspiration came directly from China. In his masterly work *Japan, A Short Cultural History*,[7] Professor Dr G. B. Sansom has dealt with the history of Japan in seven periods, throwing particular light upon the art and learning of each period. Painting was strongly influenced by Zen Buddhism. It came originally to Japan from China and was extremely subjective in character, being intended to convey thoughts and feelings. According to tradition the thirteenth-century Zen priest, Mu-shi, founded the Zen school of monochrome (painting in one colour). Visions or raptures were set down in brush or indian ink on absorbent paper or silk in an attempt to capture the expanse of space and time, of silence and inner peace. In the field of literature Zen influenced the *haiku* (the short poem of seventeen syllables), a poetic form

[7] It first appeared in 1931 and was twice revised and brought up to date, in 1946 and in 1952. (Professor G. B. Sansom has also published a book entitled *A History of Japan*, 3 vols., 1958.)

brought to perfection in the seventeenth century by Matsoeo-Basio.

The development of Japanese art has been classified into various periods. There is, for example, the Nara period (710-784), during which the art of sculpture flourished in particular. Under Emperor Shomu the largest image of the Buddha figure Roshana was executed. It was erected in the temple of Todaidji,[8] time and again partly destroyed, but restored again each time so that it still stands in this temple. The Fujiwara period (as an *artistic* period it lasted from 980 to c. 1170) is noted for having produced sculptors whose names have survived up to the present day and who are linked with special schools. There is then the Kamakura period (1192-1333) which was strongly influenced by the Zen doctrine. This teaching was also the spiritual source of the great development and considerable innovation in painting during the Muromatshi period (so called after the district in Kyoto where political and cultural life flourished, 1336-1573). The so-called Kano school, founded by the artist Masanobu in the village of Kano, led to the transition from religious to profane art.

The masks, the art of metal work, of pottery, all have their age-old history and provide a limitless field of study for art historians from all parts of the world, whose work constantly brings us another step closer to the heart of these ancient civilizations. Japan is more indebted to Buddhism than to China. Painting, sculpture, architecture, the arts of engraving and printing, even writing, came to Japan as part of the Chinese culture yet carried by Buddhism. The very first expressions of Japanese art were purely religious and bore the Buddhist stamp. Japanese history, both ancient and modern, testifies to the fact that the Japanese character can be barbaric, yet at the same time extremely tender and sensitive. That this sensitive side was more apparent – at least until the sad awakening in the last World War – is entirely due to Buddhism. A number of Buddhist priests were themselves talented artists: the reign of Joshimitsu (1358-1408) produced the artists Shubun and Dshosetsu, both of whom were priests. In the Muromatshi period several literary works were written by priests, for example, the

---

[8] Nara was then the capital, surrounded by seven large temples.

Taiheiki, a romantic and poetical chronicle, and the anonymous *Heike-monogatari*, a chronicle dealing with the fall of the house of Taira from the beginning of the thirteenth century, in which it is shown that the evil *karma* which the Tairas had accumulated as a result of their godlessness brought about their downfall. This latter work is attributed to a monk from the religious artistic centre of Hiei-san or Mount Hiei who attempted to reconcile Buddhism with Shinto and at the same time with Chinese philosophy.

In this brief sketch of the role played by Buddhism in Japan which was naturally more in the nature of a survey than a factual and speculative account, we have attempted to show that the revolution brought about by Buddhism in Japan was moral, literary and artistic. It did not entirely oust Shintoism, however, for according to the most recent data there are thirteen Shinto sects in Japan as compared with eleven Buddhist. Christianity is represented by 1,800 churches; the Protestant mission numbers roughly 210,000 believers, the Roman Catholic 120,000 and the Greek Orthodox 150,000.

We hope that we have made it clear to the reader that the essence of Japanese thought and belief is to be found in Shintoism and in Zen Buddhism. It is difficult to define the exact content of these religions with the written word since they reach man through inner revelation. The dissemination of Buddha's teaching was a triumphal progress; art and philosophy, faith and meditation lent it the power to transform the Land of the Rising Sun into a luminous centre of culture and philosophical thought.

SUGGESTIONS FOR FURTHER READING

Anesaki, M., *History of Japanese Religion*, Routledge
Hammer, R., *Japan's Religious Ferment*, SCM Press
International Congress for the History of Religion, *An Outline of Shinto Teachings*, Tokyo
Watts, A., *The Way of Zen*, Penguin

5

THE INTER-RELATION OF EASTERN RELIGIONS AND SCHOOLS OF THOUGHT

IN THIS penultimate chapter we intend to discuss the personality of a number of Chinese philosophers and to give a general outline of their systems, since they inspired and contributed to the religions already discussed. Confucianism, the doctrine of Lao-tze, Jainism, Taoism cannot be regarded as clearly defined, independent religions, although they are indispensable for a proper understanding of, for example, Shintoism and Zen Buddhism.

The thing which strikes us time and again as we attempt to penetrate the oriental mind is the recurrent, oppressive question which preoccupies the Oriental: what is the aim, the value of life? Like all mankind, the Oriental strives after happiness, but he follows a different path from the Occidental who, if he is a believer, seeks it in certainties, in a being enfolded in God's eternal protection and love. The Oriental lays the stress on self-denial, on detachment from material things, on rising above the material self, on attaining a loftier insight in order to gain inner peace and purification. What attracts us in the Oriental is his spiritual harmony (balance) and outward impassivity. We speak then, rather enviously, of 'inner refinement'. Yet this tranquil, serene outward appearance can sometimes be a cloak for boundless cruelty, which we dismiss as 'primitive'.

The Oriental expects less of life than we do. He adopts the viewpoint that half of our life is taken up by our early youth, during which we live, to a certain extent, unconsciously, and then by our unproductive old age. Of what remains half is spent in sleep and of the remaining half yet another half is swallowed up by illness, pain and grief. This leaves a period of roughly ten years during which a person can contentedly live, work and enjoy himself. Once we are born, therefore, we must accept our fate, and allow things to take their course. When death approaches we must await it quietly and accept it. Why should we bother to lengthen or to curtail life? Life distinguishes all creatures from each other, but in death they are all equal. In life there are wise men and fools, rich men and poor, and in this they differ from each other. In death they all become the same. In death man is confronted with an inexorable and predestined fate. Man must be content with the present and not worry his head about life after death. Such is, in brief, the essence of the oriental philosophy of life.

Confucius was born into a wise period. Those who considered that they had something special to communicate, travelled through the country, proclaiming their wisdom in towns and villages. They were 'travelling thinkers'. One must not overestimate these learned men, however, for there were many pseudo-philosophers among them who could in no way be considered truly wise but who were adept at giving crafty advice to rulers who sought to justify their reprehensible deeds. This, however, did not prevent the truly great thinkers from enlightening people on the problems of life or from suggesting solutions. Among these was Confucius, the full extent of whose philosophical thought was only understood and propagated after his death.

The name Confucius is the Chinese name K'ung-Fu-tze (meaning Master K'ung), latinized by Jesuit missionaries. Confucius' first name was Ch'iu (meaning a hill). He was born in 551 B.C. of an old, impoverished noble family in the State of Lu, the modern province of Shantung, in northern China. His father, Shü-liang Ho, was the governor of a south-western city where he had the opportunity to develop his great military gifts. He must have performed a number of heroic deeds which endowed his personality with a legendary renown. His chief wife had borne him nothing but daughters, although he had a son by a concubine. The child, however, was a cripple and was kept in the background. At an advanced age Shü-liang Ho married a very young woman who became the mother of Ch'iu, the future Confucius. He was three years old when his father died. He was brought up under difficult circumstances which enhanced his spiritual training, since his thoughts were not distracted by worldly pleasures and he was able to develop his talents undisturbed. These talents were many-sided, for Confucius possessed a considerable knowledge of politics and educational ideas along with his philosophical gifts. He married as a youth of nineteen and became the father of three daughters and a son (Li Po-yu). The son died before his father at a fairly early age.

The accuracy of the facts in the numerous biographies of Confucius is frequently disputed. Confucius himself never set down the details of his life, and one is forced to rely upon the accounts given by his disciples and upon the conversations with his disciples which were noted down. Without straining the truth, however, one can safely say that he held various administrative functions, that he was involved in various political developments in the State of Lu, that he acted for a brief period as governor of the town of Chung-tu, but finally fell into a sort of spiritual isolation because people failed to understand him and refused to accept his fertile ideas and honest methods of administration. The State of Lu was ruled by a duke who had little real power; this was entirely in the hands of higher officials and chancellors. When a revolution broke out in the State the duke was obliged to flee, and Confucius accompanied him. Their friendship and collaboration did not last long, however; they parted company and for about fourteen years Confucius led a roving existence with a number of faithful disciples. He journeyed from one city to another, and had strange adventures, many of which seem extremely far-fetched. He was received with great respect at many courts but he never succeeded in obtaining another high function. He then proceeded to devote himself to increasing his own knowledge and to teaching youths. A school which he founded gained great renown and was attended by many young pupils. Together they studied the Rites which indicated the correct inner and outward relationship between people. Confucius finally retired to the tranquil village of Ko-fu, where he died in 479 B.C. at the age of seventy-two. His tomb may still be found there.

Confucius did not set down his thoughts in books, nor did he leave any work behind him. The Chinese philosophers regarded books as dead things and transmitted their thoughts to their pupils who, as it were, constituted a living continuation of their ideas. These pupils often felt the need to note down recollections of or thoughts uttered by their master, but this usually only occurred years later so that there was considerable likelihood that the original thoughts were further elaborated or even supplemented by the disciples. We are thus justified in doubting the absolute authenticity of Confucius' recorded thoughts, although this, of course, detracts little from their value.

In the case of Confucius also, the tenets of his teaching were written down by disciples. They compiled three books: Analects (Lun Yu) (discussions and sayings), The Great Learning and The Middle Way. Of these three the Analects are by far the most important. They constitute a collection of sayings, remarks, answers to questions and definitions of ideas and are considered historically reliable. One finds in them many of Confucius' own words and in this way we obtain a clear insight into his mental processes.

It frequently happens that the name Confucius immediately suggests profound philosophical systems and formulae inaccessible to the untrained thinker. This, however, is not so at all; Confucius' philosophy can also be understood by the 'outsider'. In his work on the Chinese philosophers, the late Professor H. Hackmann defines Confucius' range of ideas as follows: 'Confucius was preoccupied exclusively with the problems of community life as he saw it in his own people. What interested him was man; man as he lives here on this visible earth and all his needs. He was deeply touched by the sorrows which people had to endure in that period of bloody struggle and confusion. He never concerned himself with the deeper philosophical questions concerning the origin of all life, the aim and meaning of existence, the nature and limits of our thought, in short with the problems which preoccupied so many other thinkers, especially in India and in the West. He had simply nothing to say about them.' Professor Hackmann stresses that Confucius' tenets were intended not primarily for the individual but for the social group. Although he often speaks of the individual, and lays down rules to govern the duties and actions of the individual, and although he always worked to educate the individual, his main concern is none the less always the community, the group. The individual is always judged, sometimes implicitly, sometimes explicitly, in connection with the community of which he forms a part. The demands made upon him are determined by the needs of the community, and the aim of his education is in the last instance to render him fit for this community and to teach him his proper place within it. The greatest, all-embracing community is the State, the people organized as a whole. But to Confucius the concept 'State' meant something different from what it does to us. We people of the present day – writes Professor Hackmann – regard world events as one great whole and view everything together from the viewpoint of the causal link. One thing causes another, one thing is the result of the other and everything develops according to established rules, to natural laws. Life thus becomes in fact a perpetual birth and dying, an eternal cycle of events, and 'to explain' means to us to point out the causal connection between these events. The age of Confucius viewed the world differently. For the people of his day the world was a combination of mysterious forces and it was difficult to detect the connection between them. Life was a mysterious amalgamation of interwoven organisms whose existence was determined by the influence of their qualities – viewed not as abstractions but as real forces. If the forces which belonged together co-operated, this signified prosperity; if influences which did not belong together came into conflict, this led to disturbances and decline.

Confucius regarded the State as a body with a head: the ruler. Upon this head depended the life of the entire body. Hence Confucius' statement: 'When the personal life of the ruler is irreproachable all will be well in his country even without laws, but if his personal life is evil everything goes wrong even though he enacts wise laws.' He saw the State as a circumscribed whole in which all sorts of mutually dependent

relationships and spheres of influence are in a constant state of
interaction. When they are all, each according to its own nature
and power, active in their appointed places, harmony reigns in
the State. This harmony is referred to as Tao (the [Right] Way),
in other words it is the world order in which each element, each
phenomenon works in its predestined place. Confucius considered it his destiny to restore the Tao of the State, which had
fallen into disharmony. He therefore addressed himself primarily to the young people in order to re-educate them and to
impress upon them that every person should fulfil his task as
well and as scrupulously as possible in his appointed place.
This becomes clear when we examine more closely the actions
which Confucius considers of the highest importance if the life
of the State is to remain healthy. At first sight they seem un-
important, almost incidental. He attaches great significance, for
example, to all sorts of ceremonies, such as the decoration of
the ruler's gala coach, the headdress to be worn on festive
occasions, the execution of certain melodies. In our eyes all
these are merely externals, but for him they were indispensable
if the Tao of the State were to be perfected. Music, for example,
had a mysterious and religious character; it possessed a supernatural mystery and from it emanated forces which could
benefit the State. The same was true of Li Ki, a collection of
ideas which can perhaps best be summed up by the words:
respect for ceremony and seemliness in personal behaviour.[1]
In point of fact the same rules still hold good in our modern
society: one employs higher standards in judging the outward
mode of life of an exalted personage, a ruler, a scholar, a
clergyman, than one does for the ordinary citizen. A person in
a responsible position is held more accountable for failure than
a subordinate worker. It followed, therefore, that a ruler, a
minister, anyone in a position of authority was called upon to
show himself to be virtuous and strictly to observe Li Ki. It was,
however, more a code of good manners than of good moral

[1] Lin Yu Tang points out that the Chinese word Li cannot be
rendered by an English word. 'On one extreme, it means "ritual",
"propriety"; in a generalized sense, it simply means "good
manners"; in its highest philosophic sense, it means an ideal social
order with everything in its place' (*The Wisdom of Confucius*, 1938,
p. 13). Li Ki is said to have contained 3,000 rules of conduct.

conduct. Li Ki was in Confucius' eyes of considerable value since it was the symbol of a constant communion between man and God; when interpreted as etiquette it could easily be extended to cover the relationship between man and man. The later Confucianists expanded it to such an extent that it embraced the entire culture. In Confucius' opinion the observance of good manners was an outward and visible sign of inner goodness.

One reads with some amusement that in Confucius' day 'word' threatened to lose its value, for the same is also true in our time. Our 'word' devalues rapidly, becomes worn out and weakened in meaning by the many and often misleading interpretations attributed to it. This must have been equally so in Confucius' time, for he was continually insisting that 'things should be called by their true name'. For it was becoming more and more customary to give to words and names a different interpretation from the one they originally possessed. This Confucius considered not only unworthy but even dangerous to mental balance and thus to the preservation of the State. Confucius' ideal was a static society in which any change was undesirable.

Although Confucius' wise lessons were intended chiefly for the ruling class, in order to drive home a sense of responsibility, he also addressed himself to the humble. He urged them to be content with the station in life to which they had been called, to carry out their appointed task properly; he impressed upon young people that they should honour their parents and elders. Confucius' extremely conservative teaching, which was directly contrary to the spirit of the 'new age', provoked considerable opposition and in the beginning the Confucian school was regarded with extreme suspicion. One might say that the establishment of Confucianism as a State religion only dates from the beginning of our era. Then a canon of classical books came into being which the late Professor J. J. L. Duyvendak, in his essay on the Religions of China (in *De Godsdiensten der Wereld*, I), classifies as follows: The Yi Ching, the Book of Changes, an astrological work with commentaries; the Shu Ching, the Book of History, with traditions concerning kings of certain periods and legendary figures; the Shi Ching, the Book of Poetry, a collection of folksongs, songs for use at sacrifice, etc.; the Ch'un Ch'iu, the Spring and Autumn Annals, a chronicle of the State of Lu (where Confucius was born). There are three commentaries to this book. In addition, three works on the Li Ki relating to State institutions and ceremonies such as marriage, burial and sacrifice; finally the Lun Yu, the discussions with and sayings of Confucius to which three books were added in later centuries dealing with 'The Middle Way'.

The idealization of the figure of Confucius, which appears to many excessive, only developed later. During his lifetime he was venerated as the Great Master, but by no means worshipped as a saint or a god. In A.D. 59, however, an imperial edict was promulgated in China, to the effect that sacrifices were to be offered to Confucius at fixed times, and in 630 Emperor T'ai-tsung had temples built in a number of districts throughout his entire empire, in which sacrifice was to be made to Confucius. Later the temples acquired, besides Confucius' own tablet (a flat wooden board that bears the names and years of birth and death of the ancestor concerned), the tablets of twenty-two men who had gained merit by fostering classical studies. By this time Buddhism had reached China, and the images and frescoes in the Buddhist temples probably provided the inspiration for the images of Confucius which now began to appear. People even went so far as to confer posthumous titles on Confucius; he was elevated first to the rank of duke and afterwards to that of prince.

Confucius called himself a 'mediator', not a 'creator'. He gave wise precepts and preached virtue and public spirit. The family, according to him, is a unit, a social organ, and the cult of family life is one of the central points of the Confucian doctrine. The family was the basis of society in China, at the top was the Emperor, the son of Heaven, who was the plenipotentiary of the supreme *T'ien* (Heaven), the Supreme Divine Power (God). The life of man must be built upon three fundamental virtues: sincerity, justice and respect. 'Do not do unto others what you would not have them do unto you' is an old saying but one that is still frequently heard. Confucius already employed it, although in a different formula: 'What I do not wish others to do to me, that also I wish not to do to them.'

Confucius, however, did not put his precepts into practice to the extent of loving his enemy: this he considered exaggerated and in any case impracticable. What would remain for the friend if one loved one's enemies? he asked. In his view the enemy deserves only justice; love is reserved for friends.

The whole purpose of man's life was to serve the community. In order to do this he would first have to change his disposition fairly radically; he would have to possess true humanity and neighbourly love and feel himself linked with his fellow men. There is really no necessity to remark on the similarity with Christ's doctrine; it is sufficiently obvious. And yet the element of neighbourly love, as expressed in Christianity, cannot be entirely equated with the teaching of Confucius which does not go so far as to say that all men under all circumstances are deserving of our love. Confucius considered it contrary to human nature to return good for evil. The evil doer can expect only justice, only goodness deserves goodness. To hate is just as human as to love.

How then can one attain the fullness of humanity? Through study, says Confucius, and he makes the distinction between meditation (reflection) and study. Reflection by no means always provides a solution; study, that is, the examination of documents and traditions from the past, provides the key to correct insight. Confucius was much attached to the past, regarding it as the principal and most inspiring example for the present. This sounds strange to us, since the deeds of those who lived in the past were not always the best nor did they always testify to the correct insight. Confucius, however, conscientiously examined the ideas of bygone sages and desired nothing more than to imitate their manner of life and thought most scrupulously. He believed in and loved the past and frankly confessed that he was no creator of 'anything new'.

Confucius only tackled religious problems with reluctance and preferred to avoid them altogether. Once, when he was asked what he thought of life after death, he replied: 'When one does not even know life yet, how could one know anything about death?' Confucius indeed was the very opposite of a mystic; he insisted rather on man's earthly obligations, and a

knowledge of humanity was for him an essential requirement
for adaptation to life in society.

In Confucius we find what are to us both antiquated and
remarkably progressive ideas. Woman he did not consider as
an independent being but rather as the natural complement of
the man and the mother of his children. He never spoke of
daughters or sisters but only of sons and brothers, whose rights
and duties he clearly defined. The wife must obey her husband;
if she is a widow then she owes obedience to her son. There is
no mention of the duties of parents towards their children.

Confucius had much to say, however, on mutual intercourse
between people, on friendship and on guiding the masses towards the path of virtue and tolerance. Joseph Gaer, in his
book *How the Great Religions Began*, says that Confucius had
a devoted disciple in his grandson Ch'i who did much to
propagate his grandfather's teaching. His name is not mentioned in other works, however, although they do speak of the
great masters of the Confucian school, Meng-tze (Meng the
philosopher), who was known as Mencius and lived from 372
to 288 and Shun-tze (300-230), who originally enjoyed more
authority than Mencius. Mencius summed up Confucius' teachings in 'The Five Constant Virtues': Goodwill (the desire to do
as you would be done by), Propriety (courteous behaviour
towards the people under your administration), Wisdom (knowledge and understanding must be our guide), Sincerity (be sincere in all you do, for without sincerity the world cannot exist).

Fifty years after Confucius' death it seemed as though his
teaching had perished for ever. Ts'in She Hwang-ti succeeded
in gaining absolute power and in having himself proclaimed
emperor. Although the country had had very many emperors
before him, he called himself the first emperor in order to show
that he did not recognize his predecessors. When once, in con-
versation, someone recalled the great philosophers the country
had produced, the emperor's courtiers warned against the ideas
held by these scholars who looked only to the past. Even
worse, they studied the works of men like Confucius who had
no understanding of what was new in their times. At the
insistence of his advisers the emperor decided to have all Confucius' books burned, and for many days the flames soared

high before the royal palace, devouring the books. A number of scholars, however, tried to save their copies, thus incurring the emperor's wrath. Hundreds of them suffered a horrible death. When Ts'in She Hwang-ti died a few years later a number of books emerged from their hiding places, even from the Great Wall, for many scholars had been sentenced to forced labour and sent to work on it.

Confucius' memory was restored to honour and Professor Hackmann has this to say: 'The Han dynasty (202 B.C. to A.D. 220) realized the value of his teaching for the preservation of the State and put him on a pedestal. From this time onwards he was no longer the man who pointed the way to an ideal; he himself had become an ideal.' One may probably explain the survival of Confucianism by the fact that it appealed to the common sense of the Chinese people.[2] Confucius was not an intellectual and was by no means obsessed by a thirst for knowledge beyond the bounds of what can be perceived. He sometimes spoke of God and Heaven in passing but did not dwell on either. The Chinese people were convinced that he had a divine mission to instruct in moral excellence. 'God granted him the virtue, which was not his own.' Confucius was accused by the Communists of teaching feudal and superstitious doctrines, though Mao Tse-tung has affirmed that the new culture of China is developed from the old and cannot cut itself off from the past, and has told party members that they can learn from Confucius and Sun Yat-sen as well as from Lenin. Confucius' teaching is still much respected among Chinese abroad. There he is lauded with the following words:

> You are great, O most excellent wise one,
> Your virtue is complete, your doctrine is perfect,
> Among mortal men there has been none other like you.

The name of Confucius is inseparably linked with that of Lao-tze, another of the great thinkers who moulded the beginning's of China's spiritual history. Both were the exponents

---

[2] One should bear in mind that there are several forms of Confucianism and that there is an important distinction between the Confucianism of Confucius himself and that of the first centuries after his death, at the time of the Han dynasty or the much later Neo-Confucianism.

of schools which diverged yet complemented each other. Confucius' endeavour was directly concerned with life itself, and he believed in the power which goodness exercises upon man. He wished to show his fellow men the way out of the world which had sunk into confusion and to help them to realize the good and constructive forces hidden within them. However, he came up against a wall of ill-will and impotence and had to contend with the evil inclinations which are part of human nature. He failed, and at the end of his life realized the hopelessness of the task which he had set himself. Not until centuries later would it appear that he had inspired many virtues in his people.

Lao-tze, on the contrary, felt himself caught up in the transcendental. He regarded life as an incomprehensible mystery and the only reality was for him the unknown and the unattainable. That which we think we perceive as real on earth during the brief period of our lives is a deceptive reality: 'Detach yourself from this world,' he said, 'abandon the restless urge to act which besets mankind and allow yourself to be borne along by the gossamer breath of the supreme power which is apparently powerless. Live in a higher world.'

In order to form an opinion on the different values of the respective philosophies of Confucius and Lao-tze, one would have to penetrate to the heart of their message. In his book *The Wisdom of China*, which is devoted to Lao-tze, R. B. Blakney writes that Confucius once travelled to the city of Chou to consult Lao-tze and to speak with him of bygone heroes. Lao-tze said: 'All the men of whom you are now speaking have long since gone to dust. Only their words have been preserved. When the time has come for a capable man, he rises aloft; if this does not happen he drifts about aimlessly. I have heard that canny merchants keep their goods well hidden somewhere to make it appear that they have none, and that a noble man of perfect character feigns ignorance. Give up your proud demeanour, worthy sir, your many desires, your vain conduct, your extravagant plans. They will do you no good. That is what I have to say to you.' Confucius was somewhat hurt by this treatment. He returned to his disciples and said: 'I know that birds can fly, that fish can swim and that four-footed animals can move swiftly. Snares can be laid for things that walk, nets for those that swim and bows can be used for everything that flies. But dragons? I shall never know how these ride to the sky, through wind and clouds. Today I met Lao-tse, he is like a dragon.'

Blakney considers it very probable that Lao-tze (Old Master) was a pseudonym. Lao is not a surname but an adjective meaning *old*. This would indicate that the writer of the work (attributed to him) Tao Te Ching (*The Way of Life*) was an aged man. He is said to have been born in 604 B.C. somewhere in the province of Honan and to have worked for many years as a chronicler in the secret archives at the court. His official name is thought to have been Po-yang and after his death he was called Tan. Only posterity knows him as Lao-tze.

Lao-tze would not have felt at home in our society. He shunned fame and renown, preferring to live a hidden life. He was averse to every form of vanity and spoke as little as possible. In the book Tao Te Ching he explains the concepts of Tao and Te. Tao we find in Buddhism, Zen Buddhism and also in Confucianism. As we said in our remarks on Confucius, the word means *way*. In Confucius it was the way which led to the regulation of the State and Confucius indeed spoke of the Tao of the State. Lao-tze gave a more comprehensive meaning to the concept, considering it as one of the leading forces in the world. It possessed no shape, but was of a transparent clarity, and from it proceeded all forms of life in their endless diversity. It was operative over the entire world but no one could perceive it. Te one might perhaps render as *virtue*. It was the realization of the Tao in the life of a person who keeps the Tao as his goal. Professor Hackmann defines it thus: 'To accomplish something and then withdraw, that is Te.'

We said that Lao-tze would not feel at ease in our clamorous society, but neither would we feel at ease with him. He was against too much development and would not hear of 'overloaded' education. He considered popular education dangerous for it led to people being crammed with too much knowledge which they could not absorb in any case. Let them rather lead a tranquil, true life, for all this appearance of learning only makes them discontented. He wished to give the people a reasonable material standard of living but thought that if they came to know *too* much they became unmanageable and difficult to govern. He even went so far as to argue that the people should have nothing to do with the way in which they are governed. It is none of their business and they must not meddle in such matters.

War was an absolute abomination to this gentle philosopher. Everything obtained by force of arms is in conflict with Tao. War achieves nothing, and no good can ever come of it, although he admits that war can sometimes be unavoidable as a result of 'abnormal relations'. He is no believer either in the utility of contact with other peoples. All States should be kept as small as possible and their inhabitants should think quietly of their own welfare and work for the necessities of life without aspiring to luxury. Allow them to enjoy a few simple pleasures, keep them inside their own country and in the end you will see that they have lost all desire to leave their native land. In this way all possibility of struggle and dissension is avoided and everyone leaves everyone else alone. One must admit that this is a simple solution to the international problem!

In his translation of the book Tao Te Ching – which he renders as *Way of Life* – Blakney has included a number of poems, each provided with a paraphrase. Here we find deep words of wisdom. We read that the impersonal nature of the visible world gives us the impression that it extends far beyond itself. Its end, however, is eternal and the world therefore is eternal. The Way (Tao) has the power to alleviate all harshness. If one gazes into its bottomless depths it seems that it can lead nowhere but to God's domain. The world within man reflects the world about him; the principles of both worlds are the same. Steadfastness is found only in the heart, confusion arises only in the world outside.

Taoism has been defined somewhere as 'the religion few can understand'. Lao-tze once said that one can never learn anything about Tao unless one knows all about it already! It began as a 'system of thought' and developed into a religious system. The Confucianists laid particular emphasis upon man's moral and ritual behaviour, whereas the Taoists were more concerned with the actual nature of the 'Way'; they strove for union with Tao in order to draw from it vital forces. A number of Chinese emperors who professed Confucianism officially followed the Taoist customs in secret, and it was mockingly said, though not without foundation, that many a Chinese emperor died from consuming too much of the elixir of life.

At the end of the second century of our era Taoism became organized, with a Master of Heaven or True Man at its head. He possessed the power to exorcize the devil, which he did with a variety of magic formulas which were supposed to drive out demons and sicknesses. Millions of ignorant Chinese believed in this magic and embraced the new faith out of fear, so that it rapidly developed into a popular religion. This rapid expansion can partly be explained by the fact that the Chinese had long been nature worshippers, and Taoism identified itself with nature and adopted the worship of a number of nature gods. It acknowledged a colourful company of the most extraordinary gods, with a god of the underworld, a god of ramparts and ditches intended for a walled city (he advised officials on difficult cases), also a god of wealth, a special god for the literate, a god of war (Kwan-ti); in short, the number of deities is unlimited since every river, mountain and rock, to say nothing of thunder, lightning, rain, snakes and tigers, had a separate god.

Violent disputes raged between Buddhists and Taoists in the thirteenth century A.D. The former accused the latter of having adopted their doctrine and falsified it. The Taoists lost the battle and were compelled to burn publicly many of their writings and to give back a number of Buddhist temples which they had appropriated.

A few words now about Jainism, the religious and philosophical sect in India which originated at about the same time as Buddhism as a reaction against Hinduism. The scholars, naturally, do not agree on the origin of the sect which, according to one school of thought, arose in the first centuries of our era and, according to another, did not begin to flourish until the tenth. Its founder is said to be Varahamihira, who was called Maha-vira, great hero, though some hold the viewpoint that

Gautama Buddha, the founder of Buddhism, and Gautama
Indrabhoeti, one of Maha-vira's disciples, are one and the same
person. This theory is suggested by the English orientalist,
Henry Thomas Colebrooke, one of the founders of Indian
philology, in his *Essays*. One thing is certain, however, and that
is that Jainism developed from Buddhism. The word Jain is
derived from the name Jina, victor, which was given to those
mortals who, by force of self-control and ascesis, raised themselves above the gods and revealed to humanity the true path
of redemption. According to the latest figures there are now
about 1,500,000 supporters of Jainism in India, most of them
belonging to the more prosperous sections of the community.

Jainism has two orders of monks. They live by what they can
beg, wear white robes and gain merit by suffering as many
hardships as possible. In the eyes of the Hindus, who regard
the Vedas as a divine revelation, the Jains, like the Buddhists,
are heretics since they possess their own holy scripture which
was written by their founder or by his disciples. There is, none
the less, a point of resemblance between Jains and Buddhists
which Colebrooke defines thus: 'Belief in the transmigration
of souls, together with a painful awareness of man's unhappy
lot on earth, forms the basis of the metaphysical speculation of
the Hindus. All Indian systems seek after knowledge which
will enable its possessor to escape from this pitiable condition.
The soul is in chains, in slavery; slavery brings suffering, and
good works as well as bad lead to slavery since they find their
retribution in the transmigration of the soul and in the return
of the soul to a link with an earthly and intellectual nature.
For this reason religious acts are imperfect since they grant
only a temporary release from the calamities of life. The great
secret – the philosopher's stone – is knowledge or a proper understanding of the relationship of the soul to the world or to
God. In their solution to this problem the systems diverge in a
varied multiplicity of speculations, but all have the same goal,
a sort of quietism with more or less mystical doctrines. The
adoption of one or other of these systems is the first step
towards redemption, while complete release is obtained through
meditation or abstraction.' The condition brought about by
this release is known to both the Jainists and the Buddhists as

Nirvana and from this condition no return is possible. The Jains, however, consider it illogical that at the death of a living person this same person should not enjoy the fruits of his acts on earth and thus they assume the existence of something permanent – the soul.

If, finally, we pause a moment at the figure of Zarathushtra, the founder of the ancient Persian religion Mazdaeism or Parsiism (to give it its modern name) this is because he is already mentioned in the Avesta, the sacred Books of the Zoroastrians (followers of Zarathushtra). We cannot be certain of the period in which he lived. The middle of the sixth century B.C. is usually suggested, but he could also have lived a couple of centuries earlier. Even during Zarathushtra's life legends arose which after his death became more numerous and more unlikely. His personality and his work lie hidden so deep in the tangle of sagas which have grown up around him that doubt has frequently been expressed as to whether he actually existed at all. Was he perhaps merely a mythical figure? There are sources enough for the scholars to draw upon, but they have never been able to agree on the value to be attributed to these sources. On one point, however, they are unanimous. Zarathushtra's doctrine is contained in the Avesta, the bible of the Parsis. The name Zarathushtra has given rise to endless discussion. The Greeks already began it by incorporating the word *aster* (a star) in the name Zoroaster and thus making of him a star worshipper. Much later, when Zarathushtra came under discussion, a much more straightforward explanation was suggested; *oestra* or *ustra* is a camel, which would make him, Zara, the camel driver. The name has also been regarded as a derivation of the name of the god Ahura Mazda. He is said to have been born in the north-west of Iran (or Persia), in the city of Raghai, the remains of which can still be seen in the vicinity of Teheran.

Zarathushtra originally worked as a teacher and preacher in this district and gathered a small community about him. But once again the familiar story was repeated: most of the people from his own region entirely rejected his teaching. Like Muhammad he was compelled to flee. He journeyed from place

E

to place until finally, in Seistan, in the territory of the East-Iranian tribal ruler Vistaspas, he succeeded in gaining sympathy for his teaching. Vistaspas protected him and encouraged him, aided by two learned men, the brothers Frasaustras and Jamaspa. The seal was set on their friendly relationship when Zarathushtra married one of Frasaustras' daughters, and Jamaspa took as his wife one of Zarathushtra's daughters by a former marriage. Zarathushtra is said to have died at the stake at the age of seventy-seven, but the exact date is not certain.

The late Professor J. H. Kramers has written that we must accept that the earliest part of the Avesta, the so-called Gathas, poetical sermons of considerable literary merit, are by Zarathushtra himself. In them he addresses the highest god, Ahura Mazda, and asks his help in his attempt to lead humanity to choose Truth and reject Falsehood. The supporters of truth are those who promote agriculture and protect cattle; the supporters of falsehood are those who oppress the farmers and worship false gods. At the beginning of the world there were two spirits; a good Spirit who chose Truth and an evil Spirit who opted for Falsehood. Those who chose good would gain a reward but those who preferred evil would end up in an abode of hell. The final accounting took place in the midst of fire under the most terrible torments. Fire has always occupied an important place in the worship of the Zoroastrians; their fire-temples were sanctuaries where fire was worshipped, so that in the Middle Ages they were given the still familiar name of 'fire worshippers'. Up to the present day the Parsis have temples in which the 'eternal fire' burns.

Besides Truth there also existed various 'deified ethical concepts' such as Good Mind, Devout Submission, Health and Immortality. According to Professor Kramers, Zarathushtra's preaching gave rise to a religious development in which a number of older religious ideas were incorporated. Since antiquity Mithra, the god of light, had been worshipped in Iran. He bore a completely masculine character and was thus given no goddess as consort. In later Mithraism, which was for a long time the mystery-religion which held most appeal for the Iranian people, Mithra was the redeemer from the powers of darkness. His loyalty and sense of duty made him a favourite god of soldiers.

Zarathushtra's doctrine is only comparatively monotheistic with all the powers grouped about the god Ahura Mazda. It views the spiritual world as mutually linked with the material world. Not only does the spiritual world form the background of earthly existence; it also preceded it in time. The world is thought to have had only a spiritual existence at its creation and to have acquired its material form later. At the time of the Sassanian dynasty (A.D. 226 to 651) Zoroastrianism was the State religion with its own priestly hierarchy.

As Islam's power grew the number of Zoroastrians declined; they are now reckoned at about 11,000, with the majority living in Teheran. The Parsis, those descendants of the original adherents of Mazdaeism, number roughly 100,000 and live for the most part in Bombay and western India. Iran (Persia) retains only small communities, about 16,000 to 17,000 members in all, mostly belonging to the intellectual, the well-to-do merchant and the upper classes. Even these are divided again into small sects. A number of age-old rites are still observed with considerable devotion, including placing the remains of a dead person on a special high place so that they may be devoured by birds of prey. This is in accordance with the existing precepts governing purification.

SUGGESTIONS FOR FURTHER READING

Guillemin, J. D., *The Hymns of Zarathushtra*, Murray
Lin Yutang, *The Wisdom of China*, Four Square
Smith, D. H., *Chinese Religions*, Weidenfeld & Nicolson
Waley, A., *The Way and its Power*, Allen & Unwin
Zaehner, R. C., *Dawn and Twilight of Zoroastrians*, Weidenfeld
Zaehner, R. C., *The Teaching of the Magi*, Allen & Unwin

6

JUDAISM

IN THIS last chapter, it is not our intention to write the history of the Jewish people, but merely to sketch the content of the Jewish faith. We shall thus not dwell upon periods of power and greatness, or follow the course of Israel's trials and struggle. The Jewish people can look back upon a history of many thousands of years during which it has experienced much and suffered unspeakably. It has been admired and feared, humiliated and persecuted, has fallen and risen again. At the present day it lives more intensely but perhaps more dangerously than ever, now that its existence is once again threatened. And yet the Jews have managed to preserve their unity throughout the centuries, and the State of Israel is regarded as the fulfilment of the Old Testament prophecies, in which the return of the Israelites to the land of their fathers was predicted.

The 'golden age' of the United Kingdom of Israel, the product of the unification of the tribes and governed by enlightened rulers like Saul, David and Solomon, lasted scarcely a hundred years. After Solomon's death in 933 B.C. it split into two kingdoms, one in the north which retained the name of Israel and over which nineteen kings reigned, and one to the south which was given the name of Judah and which knew twenty kings. The split was the result of the revolt of the northern tribes against David's dynasty and against the centralization introduced by Jerusalem. The kingdom of Israel with its capital Samaria continued to exist for about two centuries and was conquered in 721 by the Assyrians; Judah survived for almost a century and a half longer until Nebuchadnezzar put an end to it with the destruction of Jerusalem. The word Jew is derived from the word Yehudi – he who belongs to the tribe Yehuda (Judah). One can also find the name Hebrews in the

Old Testament: 'People on the other side', probably intended originally as contrast to the inhabitants of Canaan.[1]

The Jewish religion is based upon written and oral teaching. The written code is not set down in its entirety in the Tenach (an abbreviation of the Hebrew words, Law, Prophets and writings) but only in the first part, the Torah (Pentateuch). The scroll of the law also contains only this part. The Tenach in its entirety is extremely important for Judaism, but only the Revealed Word of God himself in the Torah is binding. This is thus not a law but a doctrine. Judaism sees in the Torah the direct dictation of God to Moses, and the sayings of the later prophets may never be in contradiction with the word of the Torah.

The oral teaching is the explanation of the written; it was originally transmitted orally and was only afterwards written down in the Mishnah (literally 'instruction').

The Jewish religion has no founder in the sense that Muhammad can be said to have founded Islam, Buddha Buddhism and Jesus Christ Christianity. Abraham and Moses can scarcely be called founders. The Ten Commandments which Yahweh gave to Moses and the setting down in concrete form of the relationship towards the Lord and towards one's neighbour are intended to assist the believer in holding his own in the midst of the dangers of this world. Judaism was the first religion in the world to teach that there is only one God. For the believing Jew the existence of God is an absolute certainty concerning which there has never been any doubt. God has always existed, there was never a time when he did not exist.

The Old Testament, however, contains no references to the nature of God. No man can see God so long as he lives on earth. When Moses in Ex. 33.12-33 asks to be allowed to see 'the glory of the Lord', the Lord replies: 'You cannot see my face, for man shall not see me and live.' Afterwards he repeats: 'You shall see my back, but my face shall not be seen.' The nature of the monotheistic doctrine automatically implies the non-recognition of other gods. The gods of the pagans thus were not considered as gods by the Jews. In the eyes of the

[1] Rufus Learsi's (Learsi is the anagram of Israel) book *The History of the Jewish People*, published in 1955, is an extremely comprehensive and modern approach to the history of the Jews.

pagans, on the contrary, it was completely understandable that
other nations and tribes should recognize other gods, since they
saw in every god a 'local' or tribal god, associated with the
local usages and customs.

The religion of the Jews sprang from the *immediate* revelation of a divine truth; thus it possesses no dogmatic framework.
This revelation, as we have said, is composed of certain laws,
rules and institutions, some of which are written down, some of
which are handed down from generation to generation. Together they make up part of the body of religious truth. There
is no question of a dogma in the strict sense of the word.
Neither can the attempts, undertaken in the course of time, to
impart a particular form be termed dogmatic decisions. This
was explained to us by the Jewish scholar whom we were
privileged to consult in writing this chapter. The decision to
change the Holy Scriptures into an unalterable *canon* was
more practical than dogmatic. This was equally true of the
writing down of the oral teaching in the Mishnah which,
together with the original written Torah, acquired the authority
of the entire Jewish philosophy of life. The Mishnah was compiled in the third century A.D. and comprises three parts which
contain legal decisions, instructions, testimonies and pronounce-
ments. After the Mishnah had acquired its final form and
authority it was zealously studied in the two prominent Jewish
centres of the time, Palestine and Babylonia (modern Iraq),
and was discussed in the schools. The short reports of these
discussions are set down in the Gemara (an Aramaic word that
also means 'instruction' [Epstein says 'completion]). There
exists in addition the Talmud (from a Hebrew root meaning 'to
study') upon which opinions are divided. According to some it
is synonymous with the Gemara; according to others it is the
Mishnah and the Gemara. There are two Talmud collections:
the Palestinian (or Jerusalem) Talmud, which originated in the
schools of Palestine, is written in a Syriac–Aramaic dialect and
is shorter and less complicated than the Babylonian Talmud
which originated in the schools of Babylonia. Its authority is
considered superior to that of the Palestinian Talmud.[2]

[2] Leiden possesses the only remaining manuscript, dating from
1289.

One of the chief contributors to the Mishnah was a famous
Jewish rabbi, the legendary Akiba ben Joseph, who closely
correlated the laws and interpretations with the word of the
scriptures. Akiba, who was martyred in A.D. 135, believed in the
possible restoration of an independent Jewish State by means
of a revolt against the Romans.

For us, the names Talmud and Torah have the most familiar
sound. The uninitiated often equate them with the Gospel of
the Christians and the Qur'ān of the Muslims. Those who
specialized in teaching Mishnah were called Tannaim; the
rabbis who discussed the words of the teachers in the Gemara
are the Amoraim (literally 'speakers'). The Babylonian Talmud
was provisionally completed c. A.D. 427 by the rabbi Ashi; a
later collection is the work of the rabbi Rabina who lived until
499.

It may thus be said that, by the beginning of the sixth
century, Judaism possessed a work in which its religious, intellectual and social life was standardized up to the present day.
From generation to generation teachers have devoted themselves to studying and explaining the texts. Thousands of
scholars have examined them, have corrected them and have
written critical commentaries about them. At the present day
study centres of modern scientific theological investigation are
to be found in Israel and in the United States. And yet it is
generally recognized that it is difficult to gain a general view
of the Talmud. It has indeed been characterized as a collection
of polemics between scribes and rabbis, debating with each
other with considerable sagacity. All sorts of subjects are discussed independently: mysticism, legends, biological and
mathematical problems. It was Moses Maimonides, the great
Jewish philosopher, who produced in 1180 a clear arrangement
and systematic classification of all the material dealt with in the
Talmud. This was the Mishnah Torah, a codex for practical
use, followed in the middle of the sixteenth century by the
Shulchan Aruch (by Joseph Karo), the codex which is still valid
for all orthodox Jews. It is also possible for the modern student
to gain some impression of the content and significance of the
Talmud; new critical editions of the Talmud have been made in
recent years, and there are several guides available.

It is a fascinating thought that throughout the centuries countless scholars have pored over the Talmud and the Torah seeking wisdom, an intensification of their faith and a directive
for their religious and social life. They were picturesque figures,
these scholars, with their long beards, the calotte upon their
heads and enveloped in the caftan. They provided artists and
sculptors with the inspiration for some of their best master-
pieces and their striking personalities imparted spiritual stature
to the whole of Judaism. Of such men it was said that 'one must
hold one's teacher in higher esteem than one's father since man
is indebted to his father for transient life, but that which he
receives from his teacher is eternal'.

The Pharisees contributed in no small measure to adding
depth to the Jewish religion. They have an unfavourable
reputation in the history of Christianity and are frequently
spoken of slightingly in the New Testament, yet they were
neither dissemblers nor hypocrites but strict observers of the
written laws. They were intractable and uncompromising people
whose thorough knowledge of religious teachings was sometimes accompanied by a certain obstinacy. Their name originated from their voluntary isolation, their custom of separating
themselves from the mass in order to fulfil God's laws in a
rigorous manner, laws which were increasingly ignored by the
masses. Not all of them were scribes, but they formed an élite
which kept to the precepts of the Torah as explained and eluci-
dated by the teachers. They lived in a sharply defined world of
laws and traditions, and every action they performed had to
correspond to God's intentions.

Now it is fairly certain that among the Pharisees, who had
united to form what amounted to a 'party', there were men who
vaunted their fidelity to the law and who prided themselves on
their piety and integrity. Even today such people are not far to
seek. Professor M. A. Beek, however, who speaks in his study
on Judaism (in *De Godsdiensten der Wereld*) of the obsession
of the Pharisees with senseless hair-splitting, writes: 'The
Pharisees strove to sanctify their lives by keeping the law. For
this reason they sought isolation and created a distance between
themselves and the people who were ignorant of this law. The
early Christian community, however, turned to the masses and

proclaimed to them, through Paul, for example, that faith grants freedom from the law. In the eyes of the Pharisees this could only lead to a cheap success among those who were not prepared to accept the discipline of God's commandments. While the Christians opted for the wide spaciousness of a life governed by faith and relying upon the disposition aroused by faith, Judaism chose the carefully outlined narrow paths of the small and great obligations which in their view all proceeded of equal necessity from the path of God.'

The Pharisees found themselves confronted by the Sadducees. These latter, also called Zadokites, considered themselves according to some as adherents of Zadok, the priest who, according to I Kings 2.35, was appointed by King Solomon to take the place of the banished Abiathar in Solomon's temple. Most people, however, consider this name to mean nothing more than followers of Zadok, one of their leaders at that time. The Sadducees, influenced by Greek culture, rejected the 'oral teaching' and were guided exclusively by the written laws. They also rejected all presuppositions concerning the eternal life which formed one of the dogmas of the Pharisees. There were no rabbis among the Sadducees. The sect consisted predominantly of statesmen, soldiers and priests. The Sanhedrin, the Jewish Council which was to condemn Jesus, was composed for the most part of Sadducees. The rabbis, on the other hand, belonged to the Pharisees, as did the Jewish historian Flavius Josephus. The historical reliability of Josephus is increasingly discounted by modern scholars. However, he is practically the only source for the study of many important periods of Jewish history.

In his work *Pharisaism, its Aim and its Method*, published in 1912, R. Travers Herford, discusses with great objectivity and completely without prejudice the attitude of Judaism towards Christianity and vice versa, and argues that in view of the sharp contrasts between Jesus and the Pharisees one might conclude that they had nothing in common. What the Pharisees regarded as religion could not be reconciled with what Jesus understood by religion. And yet they stood upon common ground, even more than is generally assumed. Jesus and the Pharisees possessed one and the same Judaism which found its expression –

according to Travers Herford – in the words of a spiritualized theism which flourished in the synagogue and in the family circle and which was taught by both Jesus and the Pharisees. What divided them was the Pharisees' mistrust of Jesus' authority, whose words acquired increasing weight among the masses. 'He taught them as one who had authority and not as their scribes' (Matt. 7.29). There was also a fundamental difference in the concept of religion, since the Pharisees regarded the Torah as the highest authority, while Jesus attributed the highest authority to the immediate contemplation of God in the mind and conscience of the individual. It might, writes Travers Herford, be closest to the truth to say that what Christ is to the Christian the Torah is to the Jews.

The Pharisees regarded themselves as the objects of God's immediate care. Nothing happens without divine approval. God sees and knows everything that man does and everything that he intends to do. Nevertheless, man possesses free will; he is obliged neither to obey nor to disobey. If he obeys then God rejoices in him; if he disobeys God is angry with him. In the first case a reward follows, in the second punishment. If he has sinned, remorse may bring about his peace with God; forgiveness is never denied to those who repent. He can always pray to God and God will always grant his prayer. There was no difference of opinion between the Pharisees and their opponents concerning God's supremacy or concerning the certainty that God is the Creator and Sustainer of all things. They believed, however, in the nearness of God and in direct contact with him. They refused to recognize any being who might in a certain sense be regarded as a second God or as a mediator between God and man (in this case, Christ).

In the Talmud exegesis reference is frequently made to the fact that God's loftiness and our belonging to him, his being far removed from us yet immediately close, are always linked. God is the Highest, but also the Closest. The ardent desire for God which is so inherent in the believing Jew only finds expression among those who are conscious of God's far-ness and at the same time of his nearness. Only the person who calls out for God invokes him. In his prayer man turns to God who 'lives on **high**' but whom he knows to be close. Here the accent is laid upon the personal relationship with God in which, however, there is a latent danger of an anthropomorphical representation of God. In order to avoid this the supernatural character of God is always stressed. Yet the danger men wished to avoid emerged at another point: the Deity could easily be transformed into an abstract, a platonic God. According to the concept mentioned in a number of writings, too much emphasis was placed upon the 'intermediary beings' situated between the distant God and man, i.e. his messengers and servants. Philosophy then created, in order to restore the link between heaven and earth, the personification, the Helper of God, the Logos, reason, understanding. The incarnate Logos is central in the Gospel of John to the belief in God, who has revealed himself in Christ. God does not exist anywhere as a person exists, but he is the origin of life as revealed in all men and in all human relationships. Faith in Judaism is exclusively the living consciousness of the Omnipresent, the sense of the nearness of God, of his Revelation which is everywhere manifest. We find it expressed in the following manner: faith is the moral gift which makes it possible to discern a firm foundation in the transient, to experience the invisible in the visible and to perceive the mystery of creation in created things in order thus to be linked with the Eternal.

The Jews speak of their faith as of 'the faith of respect for God'. He who fears and loves God bears within him the holy zeal. Judaism does not recognize original sin; sin as such does not exist but only the sins of man and of the individual. Every day the devout (pious) Jew says his morning prayer: 'My God, the soul which thou hast created in me is pure.' Faith proceeds from the words: 'God has created man after his own likeness.' This, naturally, cannot mean that God has a human form, for this would be in conflict with the prevailing prohibition of making an image of God. Deut. 4.15 says indeed: 'For you saw no form on the day that the Lord spoke to you at Horeb.' This 'likeness' refers to the soul, the sense of responsibility, man's good inclinations which raise him above the level of the animal and enable him to choose his own way and to overcome his evil inclinations. Sin is not a sort of 'original guilt' in man. It is an evil which man brings upon himself. From

God he has received the will to control his passions and to maintain a mutual harmony in the tension between the physical and the spiritual. In the Talmud one reads that God says: 'I am the same before man sinned and afterwards. . . .' The bond between God and man is never broken. Human life is usually regarded as a preparation, a hallway to eternal life, which is the true life. According to the Jewish idea man, as the image of God, belongs to a higher life and is the child of a world to come. That which is moral and good is the force and the reality of his life, and this reality is exalted above death and decay. His life continues even beyond death. The New Testament puts another view: by eternal life Jesus was not referring to a life which would never end but in the first place to a life of complete surrender to him. Surrender to the Son also implied surrender to the Father. In the first letter of John (2.17) it is written that all that is in the world is not of the Father: 'And the world passes away, and the lust of it; but he who does the will of God abides for ever.'

The Jews do not attribute the same value to a contemplative existence as do most eastern peoples. More important to them is an active participation in daily life. Physical passions are not condemned since they come from God; they should, however, be sublimated and put to the service of God's intentions. One might say that the combating of injustice and the promotion of righteousness are at the centre of Jewish teaching. To the believing Jew life on earth is important not for any material reasons, but because it gives him the possibility of doing *good*. It is well known that charity is highly esteemed by the Jews not as an act of mercy but as an attempt to restore the just balance in society.

We should like to devote a few words to messianism, the final expectation, which runs through the whole of Jewish history. This expectation originated in the very earliest times, for did not the Lord say to Abraham (Gen. 12.3): 'By you all the families of the earth will bless themselves'? These words are thought to conceal a messianic idea, and one can find this future expectation throughout the whole of the Old Testament. It emerges most strongly in Isaiah, who thought the messianic age to be close at hand. Jesus, who – and there can be no doubt about this – regarded himself as the promised Messiah, ran counter to the traditional concept of Jewish messianism.[3] He said to Pilate: 'My kingdom is not of this world' and called himself the Son of man, who had come to serve and to give his life as a ransom for many (Matt. 20.28). On the basis of Mark 9.1 Dr Albert Schweitzer has defended the thesis that Jesus was convinced that the coming of the Kingdom of God would occur during his lifetime: 'Truly, I say to you, there are some standing here who will not taste death before they see the Kingdom of God come with power.' He also found justification for this theory in the words which Jesus addressed to one of the thieves from the cross, 'Truly, I say to you, *today* you will be with me in Paradise' (Luke 23.43).

Throughout the centuries the Jews continued to hope for the coming of a Redeemer, a descendant of King David, who would restore the United Hebrew Kingdom to the glory it had possessed in the days of David and Solomon. Whereas the Christians believe in a 'beginning' (creation) and an 'end' (the establishment of God's kingdom) with at the 'middle' the second coming of Christ, there is no middle for the Jews: the end coincides with the coming of the Messiah. They rejected Jesus as the Messiah, and very many among them held the firm belief that the Prophet Elijah, who was thought never to have died, would reappear in order to prepare Israel for the coming of the Messiah. Even today many keep an empty seat at the table for Elijah when celebrating the Jewish Passover, in the expectation of his return.

To sum up one could say that the Jewish faith culminates in the concept of the entire sovereignty and power of Divine Omnipotence. Everything must be ultimately traced back to the Eternal God, nothing can exist without his power. The Spirit of God makes contact between God and man possible. God establishes contact with man through his Spirit, and this Spirit is holy because it is the Spirit of God. Reliance on the one true God, belief that the Jewish people are the 'servants of God'

---

[3] After the baptism in the Jordan 'he saw the heavens opened and the Spirit descending upon him like a dove; and a voice came from heaven, "Thou art my beloved Son" ' (Mark 1.10-11).

and the certainty that one can only serve God by obeying his commandments are the elementary foundations upon which the Jewish religion is based.

The Jewish belief, too, has had its mystic trends. The Kabbalah (tradition) was in the Middle Ages a conglomeration of philosophico-religious themes of a secret and mystical nature. Simeon ben Yochai, a tanna (teacher) of the Torah whose personality gave rise to a number of legends, is regarded as the founder of this teaching. The Kabbalah is an astounding mixture of lofty doctrines and mysterious figures and formulas which could be used to evoke hidden powers. One of the great masters of the Kabbalah was Moses de Leon (1350) who wrote the book Zohar (splendour), a compilation and elucidation of the mystical science. The Kabbalah never assumed an important place in the West European countries.

Much later, in the middle of the eighteenth century, a fascinating figure succeeded in reviving and re-animating Polish Judaism. This was Israel ben Eliezer, a stonecutter from Moldavia who gathered disciples about him at Medziboz in Podolia around 1740 and taught them that union with God is more a matter of the heart than of the mind. He did not, admittedly, reject the Talmud, but he preached that *prayer* is more important than study and revealed to his people the joy which faith conceals. He became famous as Baal Shemtob Besht (the 'master of the good name') and his followers called themselves Chassidim (the devout men). Martin Buber wrote extensively on Chassidism, recognizing in it the true religion of Judaism.

If a non-Catholic enters a Roman Catholic church or should a Roman Catholic visit a Protestant church, he will probably not feel at home there. However, the meaning of the Mass or the religious service will not entirely escape him, and there is much that will appeal to him, which he may even find moving. Even the non-believer is not completely at a loss in a Christian church.

The same cannot be said of the non-Jew entering a synagogue. He may indeed be struck by the decoration of the interior and by the externals of the ceremony, but there will scarcely be any question of a religious experience. This is not solely due to the fact that Hebrew, the 'language of Canaan', is spoken (although the vernacular is also employed in some modern services – those of Reform Judaism). This feeling of strangeness must also be attributed to the complicated rites with their symbols and diversity of vessels.

The synagogues, the meeting places of the faithful, already existed two centuries before Christ. The faithful gathered there to be read to and instructed from the scriptures by competent teachers who led them in prayer. Only after the destruction of the Temple in Jerusalem in A.D. 70 did the synagogues become the centres in which the Torah was taught. Like all churches, temples and mosques throughout the world the synagogues imparted form and content to the services dedicated to God. In the same way as the Qur'ān prescribes that the *mihrah* (recess) in the mosque must indicate the direction of Mecca, the Talmud lays down that the synagogue must face towards Jerusalem.

The synagogue, which is now more or less equated with 'church', was originally a place where religious communities met together to study the Pentateuch and for instruction and prayer. It was at the same time a social centre where the problems of the community were discussed and where justice was dispensed. One must not lose sight of the fact that Judaism has no concept of the 'Church', signifying the communion of the faithful. Orthodox Judaism considers *every* Jew bound by the religious norms by virtue of his birth. Any non-Jewish man or woman can be received into the Jewish faith – in other words, become a Jew – but the requirements are very strict. They may not seek to be converted for opportunistic reasons such as material interest or the desire to marry a Jewish partner, or for political reasons. They must give evidence of having made a profound study of the faith over a long period, of having accepted it as their religious and moral conviction and of having made it 'the desire of their hearts'. It is then the task of the Jewish ecclesiastical authority to judge whether their intentions are completely pure and whether they have embraced the faith in its deepest outlook upon life. Selection is most rigorous, and it is very seldom that admission is granted. (Any male convert must also submit to the ritual of circumcision.)

At the entrance to the synagogue, at the side facing Jerusalem, one finds the Ark, in which the scrolls of the Law or Torah are kept; in the centre stands the *bema*, an elevation from which the Torah is read aloud. During the service men and women are segregated. For a religious service to be held at least ten men above thirteen years of age must be present. The principal ceremonies are held on Friday evening, the beginning of the Sabbath, on the morning of the Sabbath and on feast days and anniversaries. During these services psalms are read and the chief prayer, the Prayer of the Eighteen Blessings (*Amidah*), is recited. The prayers are partly said or sung by the Reader (*chazzan*). Reading from the Prophets, sometimes a topical sermon and a liturgy, complete the service.

Jewish family life is strongly developed, and close ties bind the members together. There are religious and psychological reasons for this. The centuries of persecution to which the Jews have been exposed and the constant dangers which threatened them have given rise to a solidarity which has left its stamp on the Jewish community. This feeling of solidarity extends throughout the whole of Judaism so that Jews wherever they have settled in the world can to some extent be said to form a unity. On the one hand this has been the force which has held the Jewish people together, despite the Dispersion, and which has ensured its continuity up to the present day, while on the other it has led to the accusation that the Jewish people form a clan, not bound to a particular country nor to a particular nationality. Anti-Semitism has used this reproach as one of its rallying-cries and has distorted it shamefully. For in every country the Jews can be accounted among the best patriots and many of them have rendered undying service to the land of their birth or of their adoption. Their solidarity originates thus both from a certain 'community in danger' and from a common religious experience. The Jews have always been the 'few', and a minority is after all compelled to *think*.

According to the existing idea the home of the devout Jew

should be the place where the Torah is really fulfilled. This explains the many domestic religious ceremonies and the great value attached to the celebration of feast days in the family circle. Nowadays one does not often see the *Mezuzah*, the metal cylinder affixed to the doorsteps of private houses and containing a little parchment scroll with parts of the Law of Moses on one side and on the other the word *Shaddai*, the name which the patriarchs gave to God. It is also comparatively rarely that one sees the booths during the Feast of Tabernacles, although the number of booths is not small in proportion when one remembers the fatal destruction of the majority of the Jewish population in the years 1940–45.

Much has been written about Jewish feast-days, which have a profound significance and a particular atmosphere which writers and painters have attempted to recapture. Besides the religious element, emotion and aesthetics also play an important role, so that the Jewish religion, too, has its religious art. Amid great grief and suffering Judaism in its ghettoes produced its philosophers and poets, its physicians, linguists, mathematicians and astronomers. Jewish letters, alongside the Yiddish literature, Jewish sculpture, Jewish painting, Jewish music, have provided the world with some of its most glorious works. Up to the present day the world is enriched by great thinkers and artists, many of whom have never embraced the faith of their fathers, but whose works none the less still bear the vague outlines of the impress of this faith.

The old Jewish family life with its patriarchal closeness is most attractive and colourful. One of its highlights is (or was; we do not know the extent of Jewish piety in our day nor how deeply it is rooted) the Friday evening when the head of the family returns from the synagogue where he has prayed:

> Our God, and God of our Fathers, may our rest on this day
> be pleasing in thy sight.
> Sanctify us by thy commandments, and strengthen
> us with thy law.
> Satisfy us with thy goodness, gladden us with thy
> salvation, purify our hearts to serve thee in truth.

The members of his family come to meet him and all gather together around the Sabbath table after the father has sung the '*shalom alechem*' (Peace be to you) followed by the '*Esjet chajil*' (the Solomonic song of praise to women, i.e. the concluding chapter of the Book of Proverbs), an ode to his life's partner.

Sabbath begins at sunset. It is the symbol of eternal life, whereas the working days are the image of earthly life with their work and preparation for the day of rest upon which rest and peace, redemption and bliss, light and joy may be found in God. But there can be no joy without light, so that the woman of the house is given the task of lighting the two Sabbath candles. The table is laid and waiting with the two loaves, over which the benediction to the Given is pronounced. The two loaves recall the double portion which the Jews received on the sixth day in the desert since no manna fell on the seventh day. Beside the bread stands the cup of wine, the symbol of joy. 'Commemorate and consecrate the Sabbath with wine' says the precept which is followed as the cup is raised and a number of benedictions pronounced in welcome and praise to God who has sanctified his people through the Sabbath. On the wall hangs a plaque upon which is written the word *Mizrach*, the East, referring to the direction in which one should face during prayer. The washing of the hands is obligatory; it occurs frequently in Jewish life since physical cleanliness is a religious precept.

The Sabbath ends at sunset. In the evening prayer God is praised because he has separated the Sabbath from the working days of the week:

> Blessed art thou, O Lord our God, King of the Universe,
> Who makest a distinction
> Between holy and profane,
> Between light and darkness,
> Between Israel and other nations,
> Between the seventh day and the six working days.
> Blessed art thou, O Lord,
> Who makest a distinction between holy and profane.

Before work is resumed the ceremony of the *Havdalah* (meaning separation) takes place. Here the head of the household, having taken a sip from a cup of wine, pours some of it into a dish which is placed upon the table in order to extinguish the

Havdalah candle. Various prayers conclude the celebration of
the Sabbath, including a benediction to God, a prayer for the
prophet Elijah, the precursor of the Messiah whom God has
promised to Israel, and a prayer for God's blessing on the week
just begun:

> Sovereign of the Universe,
> Father of mercy and forgiveness,
> Grant that we begin the working days
> Which are drawing nigh unto us, in peace;
> Freed from all sin and transgression;
> Cleansed from all iniquity, trespass and wickedness;
> And clinging to the study of thy Teaching,
> And to the performance of good deeds.

In former days there must have been something painful about
the end of the Sabbath since it was regarded as a return to cold
reality, to the scorn and contempt, the humiliation and the
mockery to which the Jewish population was exposed in the
daily struggle for existence.

Besides the many ecclesiastical ceremonies, the Jewish
religion celebrates a number of feastdays. These are Purim,
Passover and the Feast of Weeks, New Year, the Great Day
of Atonement, the Feast of Tabernacles, the closing feast: the
Joy of the Law and the feast of Dedication. At Passover the
Seder (home-festival) or *Seder*-evening is celebrated introducing
the spring festival of freedom and redemption, the evening on
which the Jewish family dedicates its home as a temple in
order to offer thanks to God in a sober ceremony which recalls
the miraculous exodus from Egypt. At this time the medieval
ghetto-dweller forgot his sufferings for one evening and was
transported into the historical past. On that evening every
hungry, needy or lonely person could sit down to table in a
family circle. Four times in succession the head of the household held aloft the cup of wine in memory of the words with
which God proclaimed to the fathers the hour of freedom: 'I
shall deliver you, save you, redeem you and accept you as my
people.'

In order to gain a better idea of the religious significance of
these feasts and in order to bring out their pronounced family
character, let us pause a while at the principal festivals.

With the feast of Purim, which is celebrated on the fourteenth day of Adar, the twelfth month of the Jewish year, ancient Judaism commemorated the divine deliverance from the power of Israel's evil enemies. The feast is based upon the Book of Esther which tells of Haman, the favourite of Ahasuerus (or Xerxes) the persecutor of the Jews, who met his death on the gallows which he had prepared for Mordecai. It is a joyful festival consisting of prayers of thanks to the Almighty for his unexpected deliverance, readings from the stirring story from the Book of Esther, the exchange of gifts and the giving of alms to the needy. Now the Talmud is said to contain the words of a wise man called Raba who is purported to have said that on the feast of Purim the wine must flow freely so that at last one can no longer distinguish between the cry 'Accursed be Haman and blessed be Mordecai'. This exhortation, however, never found much favour among the Jews, even from the very beginning, for they have never been a drinking people. Special care is devoted to the meal, however, and it does occasionally happen that the feasters do so much justice to the accompanying wine that a saying arose: 'as tight as at Purim'. The appetite was whetted to the utmost since the day before Purim was 'the fast day of Esther' upon which one was obliged to refrain from all food and drink. Small companies of actors went from house to house giving short performances and singing songs with zither accompaniment. The evening was filled with merriment and jollity which, however, was always kept under control.

The feast of Passover is, so far as the Jewish religion is concerned, an extremely important festival.[4] There is some dispute

[4] In connection with the disquieting tension existing at the present between Jews and Arabs, it is perhaps important to refer to the phrase with which every Jewish Passover meal begins: 'This year here, next year in Jerusalem, this year as servants, next year as free men' expressing the longing for a definite home. The custom of pouring out a few drops from the cup of wine in the Seder evening ceremony symbolizes the universal brotherly love of the Jews. For Israel's Wise Men taught: 'When God's angels wished to join in Moses' song of triumph at the Red Sea God cried out to them: "The creatures of my hand suffer death by drowning and still you wish to sing a song!"'

among modern scholars concerning the origin of the word paschal. The scriptures themselves associate the word with *pesach* which means 'to limp, to jump over'. In connection with the deliverance from Egypt it signifies that God 'passed over' the houses of the children of Israel in order to spare them during the death of the first-born. Among the shepherds the year's new crop of lambs was celebrated.

The famous Elephantine papyrus contains instructions for the celebration of this feast dating from 419 B.C. The Old Testament mentions the first Passover in commemoration of the exodus from Egypt (Ex. 12 ff.) and the first celebration held in Jericho in the new fatherland under Joshua (Josh. 5.10). The New Testament tells of Christ's last Passover in Jerusalem (John 12.1). After the destruction of Jerusalem the sacrificial service lapsed and the ritual acquired a significance such that the emphasis could only be laid upon the regulations concerning the eating of the *matzoth*, the unleavened bread, and the *maror*, the bitter herbs.[5]

According to the Mosaic Law the Pentecost or Feast of Weeks – so called because it is celebrated seven weeks after Passover – derives its significance from agriculture. It is the feast of the 'first fruits', in particular of wheat. A quantity of the new barley has already been offered up as a thanksgiving on the second day of the Passover feast. Now, fifty days later, two loaves are dedicated to the Lord as the first fruits of the harvest. Yet the significance of the Pentecost feast is not exclusively an incitement to gratitude towards him who feeds and sustains all his creatures. The day of celebration – the sixth of Siwan, the third month (May–June) – coincides with the anniversary of the birth of Israel's religion, the Revelation at the foot of Mount Sinai. During the course of Israel's exile the idea of the harvest festival has faded into the background and

---

[5] It is indeed most unbiblical that in our day the Matzos are considered a fashionable delicacy and – in a small version – frequently served with cocktails. The Jew, however, sees nothing extraordinary in this, for every article, every action can be consecrated. Unleavened bread, scrupulously prepared according to the regulations and placed upon the Seder dish, over which the special benedictions are pronounced, acquires biblical, divine value. Otherwise, this same bread is just ordinary food.

the main burden of the festival rests chiefly upon the commemoration of this Revelation. Accordingly, in the synagogue
liturgy, the day is called not the 'day of the first fruits' but the
'day of the lawgiving'. The rabbis then proclaim the words of
the scriptures: 'Today the Lord commands you' since every
day is a day of lawgiving upon which the Lord commands us
anew to practise the principles set down in his teaching. When
the Ark is opened, the Reader takes the scroll of the Law and
says:

Blessed be he who in his holiness gave the Law to his people Israel.

Then the whole congregation joins him in the affirmation:

Hear, O Israel: the Lord our God, the Lord is One.
One is our God; great is our Lord; holy is his name.

The Reader then calls to the congregation:

Magnify the Lord with me and let us exalt his name together.

During the feast of Weeks the synagogue is decorated with
plants and flowers. During the service the sacred scroll is taken
from the Ark so that the Reader may recite from it the chapter
dealing with the event of the Revelation on Mount Sinai. (The
Law is read on every Sabbath and Feastday.)

One of the greatest, perhaps indeed the greatest of all Jewish
feasts, is the Day of Atonement, Yom Kippur. It owes its
origin, not to any historical event, but to the spiritual life of the
Jews, springing as it does from the awareness of the intimate
relationship between God and man. The (Great) Day of Atonement falls at the end of a ten-day period of penitence which
concludes the New Year feast. It is based upon the purification
rites which cleanse the individual of the stain of sin. Since
there is no person on earth who has never erred and sinned,
each one is granted the opportunity to free himself from sin,
to purify himself and to return to the path of devotion and
duty. 'And it shall be a statute to you for ever that in the
seventh month, on the tenth day of the month, you shall afflict
yourselves and shall do no work, either the native or the
stranger who sojourns among you; for on this day shall atonement be made for you, to cleanse you; from all your sins you

shall be clean before the Lord' (Lev. 16,30). In ancient Judaism Yom Kippur was considered the highest perfection and moral purity attainable by man and the feast retains its profound significance up to the present day. The call of the Day of Atonement is addressed not only to the Jew but to every man as a moral being. Love and peace are the dominant themes of this day. On the evening which precedes a day of fasting (called the Kol Nidre after the first words of the prayer with which the ceremony begins) the synagogue is entirely filled. The house of God is brilliantly illuminated with candles burning along the walls in memory of the dead. The majority of the worshippers are robed in white garments and wear thin cloth slippers instead of leather shoes.

Finally there is the feast of Dedication (of the temple), Chanukkah, which is celebrated in December in memory of the sombre period in Israel's history under the yoke of the Syrian tyrant Antiochus Epiphanes. He attempted to eradicate Judaism and forcibly to convert the Jews to paganism until Judas Maccabeus, son of the priest Mattathias, joined battle with him and with a small army, guided by God's hand, succeeded in defeating the Syrian legions. He entered Jerusalem, purified the temple which for three years had been used for sacrifice to Zeus and restored to honour the service to God. According to tradition, when the great candlestick was relit one little jar of oil was found which had escaped destruction. The miracle then occurred that, although the little jar contained only sufficient oil to keep the sacred light burning for one night, this quantity was sufficient to keep the candlestick alight for eight days.

The Chanukkah, also called the Feast of the Maccabees, lasts for eight days. Each evening one candle is lit on the candlestick until on the last evening it shines out in full splendour. In devout Jewish homes the Chanukkah lamp before one of the windows recalls the eternal truth that the power of truth and right is exalted above any violation and expresses the firm conviction that the pure concept of God – the source of all moral uplift – will one day spread throughout the whole of mankind.

Festivities of a more intimate nature are the *Bar Mizvah* celebrations when a boy completes his thirteenth year and is confirmed in his religious duties and privileges. He is then

considered an adult in the religious sense and enters the synagogue as such for the first time. On returning home he will, if
he is sufficiently gifted, discuss for his assembled family and
friends a fragment from the Talmud which he elucidates, if
possible, in his own manner.

Historiographers of the Jewish people accept the year A.D. 70
as the date on which the history of this people assumes a distinctive character. In that year the Roman legions ravaged
the whole of Palestine and went on to destroy the Temple.
The inhabitants were dispersed to every known corner of
the earth. In his book, *The History of the Jewish People*,
which we have already mentioned, Rufus Learsi states that
from this time onwards the historiography of the Jewish people
also acquired a different character. 'It must follow the Jews to
all parts of the earth. Moreover, from now on the history of
the Jews lacks all those factors which are so familiar to us from
the history of every other people: the display of power by
kings and conquerors, advancing armies, battles and victories.
The heroes of Jewish history are deprived of all that external
glamour associated with an exalted worldly position and with
wealth which so easily appeals to the imagination. The Jewish
heroes are sages and scholars, poets and dreamers, martyrs,
mystics and saints. From this time onwards Jewish history has
no equal in the annals of the nations.'[6] It is a history of endless
suffering, of martyrdom and exile, but also of growth and prosperity, always followed, however, by new persecutions cul-
minating in the massacre during the second World War. Even
the brightening dawn, full of hope which we witnessed in the
birth of the Republic of Israel, has been obscured by many
dark clouds over this young country.

Judaism is divided into the Orthodox (traditional-historical)
and the Reformed or Liberal groups. The latter distinguishes
between eternal and transient truths in scripture and tradition
and has set about re-interpreting certain precepts, sometimes
annulling them in order to achieve conformity with modern
social concepts. This is also intended to make the synagogue

[6] Learsi's work is unfortunately unavailable to the present translator, the passage quoted here is our retranslation.

services more comprehensible and attractive. It is clear that the non-acceptance of the binding nature of an unbreakable tradition is judged differently by different people. Circumcision, for example, may be declared obligatory by one Liberal rabbi and rejected by another. Opinions also differ on so-called 'mixed marriages' and the admission of non-Jews to Judaism. There is thus hardly any question of religious collaboration between the two groups; their disagreement concerns fundamental questions of faith and philosophy.

The Jews were granted many liberties, yet they never entirely lost their *apartheid*. This explains why, through the ages, the 'longing for Zion' persisted strongly among the Jews and has become in our era a movement with a great driving force.[7] The attempts made in the nineteenth century to establish colonies in Palestine were the beginning of the Zionist Organization, founded in 1897 by Theodore Herzl. His infectious enthusiasm and moral prestige gave to the movement fixed lines and a programme aimed at setting up a Jewish republic in Palestine. Since this was impossible for the time being the British government proposed to establish a Jewish colony in Uganda (Africa). Herzl did not immediately reject this proposal but wished to study the possibilities. He met with powerful opposition within his organization which continued even after his death in 1904. The new leaders clung to the idea of settling in Zion, which led to the resignation of those who advocated setting up a colony elsewhere. Under Zangwill they founded the Jewish Territorial Organization, but this organization proved to have little staying power.

Zionism had to endure considerable conflict within its ranks as each particular group, most of which were politically organized, strove to impose its policy. The chief opponents to Zionism as a Jewish national revival movement were the (extreme) Orthodox and the (assimilatory) Reform Jews. Supporters of colonization in Palestine, Jews faithful to the Law and political progressives carried on a mutual struggle in the Zionist World

[7] Zion, which probably means 'citadel', was originally the steep rock on the southern point between the Valley of the Cedron and the Tyropoeon near Jerusalem. It is mentioned in Isa. 10.24. Later the name Zion was identified with Jerusalem.

Organization and founded separate organs. Meanwhile money continued to flow in from America and England, where Jews displayed an extraordinary generosity in the Jewish cause.

The first World War was to lead Zionism a little way along the road towards the goal which it had set itself. Its leader at that time, Professor Chaim Weizmann, succeeded in gaining the consent of the British government for the setting up of a Jewish 'National Home' in Palestine. The Balfour Declaration of 1917 was sanctioned by the League of Nations, and this was the beginning of the setting up of the Jewish State of Israel which was proclaimed in May 1948 amid bitter struggles, setbacks, distress and anguish.

The history of Zionism has been stirring in the extreme. It is not exclusively political and economic but has a clearly religious and idealistic background. The last chapter of this history has not yet been written, and the State of Israel, whose political and cultural development has aroused the admiration of a large part of the civilized world, is now more than ever menaced.

It is with some hesitation that we pause now to discuss anti-Semitism, not only because it is one of the most shameful expressions of racial hatred, a mania, but also because it conjures up memories of horrible persecutions and inhuman cruelties. Until the end of time it will remain a psychological enigma how it was possible during the second World War for six million Jews to be scientifically 'liquidated' in the centre of Europe while civilized humanity continued to live on afterwards, rapidly recovering from the shock and scarcely admitting to any feeling of shame and eternal infamy. And yet our study of the Jewish religion would be incomplete if we failed to mention anti-Semitism which not alone has led to terrifying excesses, but in many countries has made its influence felt upon economic, political and social life. Although hatred for and defence of the Jews can be traced back to antiquity, the term anti-Semitism only emerged at the end of the previous century. Wilhelm Marr is said to have used it for the first time in 1879 in his *Antisemitische Hefte*. Originally, however, anti-Jewish reactions bore a predominantly religious character, while in our day they tend rather to be economic, with racial antagonism as a pseudo-scientific motivation in the background. We all realize that extremely subjective emotional considerations such as social and economic jealousy, group hatred, and not always explainable psychic processes in the human subconscious are, even more than religious intolerance, responsible for the effects which we all know only too well. In the Book of Esther Haman says to King Ahasuerus: 'There is a certain people scattered abroad and dispersed among the peoples in all the provinces of your kingdom; their laws are different from those of every other people and they do not keep the king's laws, so that it is not for the king's profit to tolerate them.'

But anti-Semitism was constantly changing and showed a different face in every distinct period. At the time of the Greek supremacy the Jews were resented because they segregated themselves in their religious life and did not subscribe to the Hellenistic cultural ideals. In the Roman period political factors emerge: the Jewish revolt became a threat to the Roman imperium. In the Middle Ages, wars of religion, ecclesiastical struggles, none of these spare the Jews, who are often used as the scapegoats for others' discontent. And even the age of so-called 'emancipation', which brought the Jews a certain measure of equality, created the distorted image of 'the Jew' as so often presented to the emotional masses, even in our day: the usurer, the unfair competitor, the man without a country. In a number of countries the Jews were relegated to the status of second-class citizens, suffering exclusion, pogroms, scorn and contumely. If we are to believe the remarks of various present-day Jewish writers and publicists – and there is no reason not to do so – the murder of six million Jews between the years 1940–45 has not put an end to anti-Semitism. On the contrary, in a number of countries it is still very widespread, if not on the increase.

In conclusion we should like to stress the point that the Jewish concept of God refers especially to the relationship between God and the people as a whole and that 'the Lord' cannot be disassociated from the Law, the Torah. The God of the Christians, on the contrary, is more concerned with the relationship to the 'elect' who are not confined to one particular people. He is also more concerned with personality than with the whole as a whole and he is, if not fully, at least in principle, capable of being thought of apart from law or commandments. He grants grace (in Christ) independently of the question of law and commandments. A shift in concepts and values has taken place so that the Christian concept of God now differs from the Jewish, especially since the latter clings firmly to the law from which the former has been freed.

The people of Israel rejected Jesus of Nazareth, although he was one of Israel's sons. The first preachers of Christianity were Jews just as the first Christians were Jews, and the Old Testament was the Holy Scripture of the early Christians. Their interpretation of it, however, differed so widely from that accepted in the synagogues that they broke away and founded their own synagogue. This was the origin of the Christian community, and it was only much later that it acquired this name.

SUGGESTIONS FOR FURTHER READING

Cohen, A., *Everyman's Talmud*, Dent
Danby, H., *The Mishnah*, Oxford
Epstein, I., *Judaism*, Penguin
Roth, L., *Judaism*, Faber
Schneider, Peter, *Sweeter than Honey*, SCM Press
Simpson, W. W., *Jewish Prayer and Worship*, SCM Press

INDEX